BLIND CORNERS

ADVENTURES ON SEVEN CONTINENTS

BY GEOFF TABIN

FOREWORD BY
SIR EDMUND HILLARY

ICS BOOKS, Inc.
Merrillville, Indiana

BLIND CORNERS
Copyright © 1993 by Geoffrey Tabin
10 9 8 7 6 5 4 3 2

Printed in the U.S.A.

Published by:
ICS BOOKS, Inc
1370 E. 86th Place
Merrillville, IN 46410
800-541-7323

Library of Congress Cataloging-in-Publication Data

Tabin, Geoffrey.
   Blind corners : adventures on seven continents / by Geoffrey
Tabin.
      p. cm.
   Includes index.
   ISBN 0-934802-03-3 : $24.99
   1. Mountaineering. 2. Mountains--Difficulty of ascent.
I. Title.
GV200.T33   1993
796.5'22--dc20   93-28138
                                                CIP

Foreword

GEOFFREY TABIN'S STORY is an astonishing mixture of wild adventure and the overcoming of formidable challenges. One cannot help feeling that the major battle is always with himself. He has an incredible desire to stretch himself to the utmost—almost one feels beyond his natural abilities. But somehow with considerable courage and great determination he nearly always achieves his objective despite frostbite and exhaustion and returns safely to the bottom of the mountain.

Geoff has climbed Mt. Everest up the South-east ridge and almost succeeded on the formidable East Face. But many of his greater efforts have been in the remote and inaccessible parts of the globe. He has climbed new routes on Mt. Kenya near the equator and battled his way through the jungles of Irian Jaya to reach the summit of Carstensz Pyramid. He has climbed the isolated summit of Mount Vinson in the Antarctic.

Geoff has a vast respect for Dan Reid who died on Mount Kenya in September 1991—and rightly so. I met Dan Reid when I joined his team for the first climbing exploration of the Kangshung Face of Mt. Everest and we subsequently became friends. I also first met Geoff on this same trip. Dan was an astonishing man both as a climber and a human being. In a way Dan was a role model for Geoff. They were both incredibly determined and a little crazy. They both permitted no challenge to stop them from reaching their goals—but took enormous risks in their achievements.

Geoff is a strange conglomeration of success and brilliant failure. He has met many strange personalities and seems to have enjoyed them all. But there is no questioning his courage and determination.

Sir Edmund Hillary

Introduction

This book began as a chronicle of my climbing to the highest point on all seven continents. However, the project evolved to encompass a wide range of adventures that include my experience with the Oxford Dangerous Sports Club and the invention of Bungee Jumping; spending time with Stone Age natives of the Dani tribe in Irian Jaya, New Guinea; hunting and gathering with Mbuti Pygmies in the Ituri Forest of Zaire; and the adventures of a Sherpa in America. The climbing stories include three chapters on Mount Everest. I was with the American teams that made both the first exploration and then the first ascent of the largest, steepest, and most difficult side, the Kangshung, or East Face, of the world's highest mountain. These expeditions constituted a breakthrough in the level of technical difficulty achieved thus far in Himalayan climbing. I later returned to Mount Everest and personally reached the summit on a team which also placed the first two American women on top of the world. This happened during the first year that the mountain was opened to multiple teams from different countries. The result was an amazing array of records, several dramatic rescues, and an unparalleled number of deaths.

Several of the stories have been previously published as magazine articles and stand on their own. I have attempted to tie the climbs and journeys together in a way that explains how I progressed, both physically and mentally, as a mountaineer and as a person. I was fortunate to have had good luck in obtaining sponsorship and grants, as well as having been invited on well-funded expeditions. But, "luck" is often the result of working hard and training to be ready when the time comes and can be "made" by putting yourself in the path of opportunities. My life changed dramatically, several times, when I turned blind corners, uncertain of the consequences, knowing I couldn't go back. The major purpose of this book is entertainment. If there is a message to these stories, it is to follow your dreams and maximize your life. Namaste!

Geoff Tabin,
January 1993, Providence

Acknowledgments

I am grateful to many people for their help and input on this book. Julian Bach and Tom Todd helped get the project started. Phil and Marcia Lieberman, George Lowe, and Brad Werntz read rough drafts and gave helpful input. David Bodnick provided computer assistance, and Holli Cosgrove, my editor at ICS Books, did a wonderful job of polishing the final draft.

Rick Telander, Ken Banta, Nanette Varian, and John Harlin gave valuable advice on sections of the book that were previously published as magazine articles. Some of the stories appeared in *Playboy, Penthouse, Summit, Climbing, The American Alpine Journal, Trilogy,* and *Outside,* and I thank these journals.

I appreciate the support of my family and closest friends who stood, and continue to stand, by me during my adventures. In particular I want to thank my parents, Julius and Johanna Tabin, my brother, Cliff Tabin, and Beth Peterson.

I also owe a debt to all of the great adventurers who went before me, inspired me, and showed me the way. Finally, I extend my gratitude to all of my climbing partners and companions who shared my journeys, both those named in this book and those of you who are too boring to mention . . .

Dedication

To the memory of Dan Reid: an inspiration and a friend.

ﻉ

Contents

Quest for Adventure

"SAY, GEOFF, WANNA CLIMB the North Face of Carstensz Pyramid?" I knew that in order to climb the two-thousand-foot, sheer rock wall to the highest point between the Andes and the Himalayas, we'd have to trek through dense jungle inhabited by the cannibalistic Dani tribesmen, among the most primitive people on earth. I also knew that because of terrorist activity, the Indonesian government had closed all access to the region of Irian Jaya, New Guinea, where the mountain is located. Finally, I didn't have enough money for the airfare to Jakarta, let alone to Irian Jaya. It didn't take me long to reply. "Yes!"

My friend Johnny Petroske characterizes his need for great adventures as "feeding his rat." I know what he means. Floundering, way over my head, calms my wanderlust for a while. But inevitably, a gnawing starts in my gut. It gets stronger and stronger until the only thing I can do is set out in search of yet another wild adventure. My rat will be temporarily sated. But he always returns, fatter and more demanding.

I like a good adventure. The satisfaction of turning blind corners, relying on my wits and skills to succeed is, to me, the essence of adventure. In our mechanized world of processed food, electric socks, and in-flight entertainment, real adventures can be difficult to find. The expanding "adventure travel" industry offers exotic and sometimes strenuous trips all over the world. But they do not offer adventure. Your guide makes the decisions and ensures your safety. Pay your fee and enjoy the ride—in our litigious society, the outcome must never be left in doubt. You will see tigers and mountain peaks, but you won't get the feeling of accomplishment and joy that comes from doing it yourself. Then again, if you don't take a risk, you won't get hurt. Adventure, by definition, risks failure.

Society evolved to protect us from adventure. Thomas Hobbes wrote that life in the state of nature is "nasty, brutish, and short." For example, in the Masai tribe of Africa, very few warriors seek adventure vacations. After a hard week fending off leopards with their short spears, they prefer to unwind in a nice quiet hut with plenty of fresh urine, cow blood, and milk to drink. However, the Masai do send their children out to kill a lion as part of a rite of manhood. Austrian explorer Heinrich Harrer said, "No man can summon all his strength, all his will, all his energy, for the last desperate move, till he is convinced the last bridge is down behind him and there is nowhere to go but on." Adventure tells you what you are capable of in ways that our civilization can't encompass.

One can only guess at the last words uttered by Bill Dunlop, a truck driver from Portland, Maine. Dunlop set out in July 1983 to discover his limits by circumnavigating the globe in a nine-foot sloop, and was last seen somewhere in the South Pacific in June 1984. He is presumed dead. Bill exemplifies the fine line that can exist between adventure and suicide.

When I agreed to join climber Bob Shapiro on an illegal excursion to scale the death wall in the middle of the jungle, I had spent seven years honing my rock and ice climbing skills, had acquired new route experience on the equatorial rock faces of Mount Kenya, and was familiar with Indonesian bureaucracy as the result of a month of wandering in Java and Bali. Bob was the perfect partner. In addition to being a superb mountaineer, he had excellent third-world jail experience. So even though I couldn't predict exactly what obstacles and dangers lay around the next turn, I foolishly thought it was likely that together we could surmount them.

One of my favorite parts of any adventure is the moment I become committed to it. There is a heady mix of tension, excitement, and fear. Then, incredible things start happening as a cascade of unexpected events propels me into the mess of my own design. I have a deep respect for Goethe's couplet: "Whatever you can do, or dream you can, begin it. / Boldness has genius, power, and magic in it." Word of our plans spread, and grants began to materialize from exploration and climbing foundations.

We were cruising. We had an objective that we could conceivably meet and that would push us to our limit, and we were now able to afford it. Mistakes in calculating these basic considerations can be costly. Ask Warren Pearson. A middle-aged man with a cardiac condition, Pearson decided to sail solo to Antarctica. For four years he secretly read everything he could about seamanship and the South Pole. Meanwhile, he spent $40,000 building a boat, fearing all along that if his wife found out she would veto the trip because of his ailing heart. Finally, in 1985, with no hands-on sailing experience, Pearson set out from Australia in a thirty-seven-foot ketch bound for Cape Denison, Antarctica. In the first minor storm, he lost his engine and rudder. Sixty miles from shore, his boat floundered and sank, and Pearson was scooped up by a passing freighter.

I had the ideal teammate in Bob—our climbing skills were similar and I knew him well enough to know I could count on him in times of stress. This was the best-case scenario and I did not have to resort to H. W. Tilman's approach. The taciturn British explorer who crossed Africa alone on a bicycle in 1933, and reached twenty-eight thousand feet on Mount Everest wearing tweeds in 1938, claimed that any enterprise that could not be planned on the back of an envelope should not be done. When he needed a crew to sail to the Arctic in 1957, Tilman found his shipmates by placing an ad in the London Times that read, "Hands wanted for long voyage in small boat; no pay, no prospects, not much pleasure."

Adventures can also result from conceiving new ways to tackle old problems. Larry Walters received an F.A.A. citation for violating controlled-airspace laws after he soared to sixteen thousand feet in a lawn chair rigged with forty-two helium-filled weather balloons. Using a pellet gun, the intrepid Walters popped the balloons, one by one, to engineer his safe return to terra firma. This spirit comes from the same vein as Thor

Heyerdahl, who sailed a balsa-wood raft called the *Kon-Tiki* four thousand miles from Peru to Easter Island. Adventures that delve into the unknown have allowed people to fly, explore outer space, and plumb the ocean's depths. The pioneers of these new ideas have traditionally been called insane and suicidal by the general populace, before they have proven that their dreams can be achieved.

Facing the unknown, head on, fuels additional curiosity that benefits all areas of life. Following the flow of an adventure can help turn life's misfortunes into opportunities. Heinrich Harrer was a young mountaineer from Austria when he climbed the North Face of the Eiger in 1938. Hitler hailed this first ascent of the "death wall of the Alps" as proof of Aryan superiority, and Harrer became a national hero. But Hitler decided it was important for the "fatherland" to have the altitude record, which then belonged to H. W. Tilman, who had ascended 25,800-foot Nanda Devi in the Himalayas in 1936. A German Himalayan expedition was organized to climb 26,400-foot Nanga Parbat, with Harrer as a lead climber. While the team was trekking through British-ruled India, World War II broke out, and the Germans were arrested and placed in a prison camp. Harrer then moved on to a much greater adventure. First he tunneled out of jail. Then he fled, without equipment, over 21,000-foot Himalayan passes into Tibet, where disguised as a Sikh, he eventually reached the Forbidden City of Lhasa. Harrer became one of the few Westerners to reach the Tibetan capital since Francis Younghusband had entered by force in 1903. He rose from being a destitute vagabond to tutor for the fourteen-year-old Dalai Lama, remaining as a modern Connecticut Yankee in King Arthur's court for seven years. He brought his practical knowledge of Western civilization to the isolated Tibetans while learning about their culture and exploring uncharted mountains. Adventure stems from the state of mind that says, "I want to see what is around the next turn."

Bob and I thought that we had everything under control for our journey to the Carstensz Pyramid. We were joined by Sam Moses, a reporter from *Sports Illustrated* magazine and a serious climber. In Jakarta, we obtained permission to fly to Jayapura, the center of government in Irian Jaya, and amassed letters of recommendation from the American ambassador, the Indonesian Olympic Committee, and the minister for Irian Jaya affairs, each with a fancy letterhead. We expected to plunk the impressive stationery down in front of the local officials and immediately be issued a *Surat Jalan,* or permit to visit the island's interior.

Unfortunately, upon reaching Jayapura, we found that we had only succeeded in making ourselves too important for anyone to risk their career on giving a Surat Jalan to dignitaries to visit an area where they would certainly die. The Indonesians had been engaged in low-level warfare with the Dani tribe for several years: The Javanese occasionally got excited and machine-gunned a few Dani, who retaliated by blow-darting stray soldiers. Bob and I had been told by missionaries that "round eyes" are relatively safe. We tried to convince the local officials that we would be responsible for our own asses, but to no avail. The chief of police said that he needed permission from the mayor, who said that he needed permission from the military commander, who in turn needed permission from the chief of police.

We were at a roadblock of the type that can either make or break an adventure. The more frequently I have landed in situations where the choices are to think fast on my feet or sink, the better I have become at sizing up the options. For role models on how to handle these situations I look toward the British Burgess twins. They can quick-think their way out of jams better than anyone I know—maybe because they tend to get into more sticky situations than anyone else. Wearing long blond Prince Valiant haircuts and standing an imposing six foot three with identical well-defined musculature, Adrian and Alan Burgess are a well-known sight from Lima to Katmandu. They have been traveling and climbing full-time for twenty years with no visible source of income. But many of their wildest adventures have taken place off the slopes. Recently, the pair were descending from a difficult ascent of Fitzroy in Patagonia when they were pinned down for a week by a storm and ran out of food three days before it was safe to leave their ice cave. Returning to base camp, they discovered that they had been robbed. All of their food was gone. The emaciated climbers were still two days' walk from the nearest town when they saw a flock of sheep. While Adrian started building a fire, Alan grabbed an ewe. Before reaching camp, a gaucho with a rifle rode up on him.

To be caught red-handed in a lawless land stealing another man's animal meant it was sink-or-swim time. Al quickly dropped his pants, secured his grip on the sheep's sides, and pressed the animal back into his groin. Keeping his head down, Al thrust his pelvis back and forth to simulate bestial sex until the horseman's angry voice went silent and, after what seemed to be an eternity, changed to laughter. Burgess kept the motion going until he heard the giggling gaucho ride away. Then he and his twin had dinner.

My party did not have to act quite so quickly or spectacularly. We had time to explore all of our possibilities. We thought that once we were out of Jayapura, we would be safe from government restrictions. However, without the proper papers, we couldn't even leave the airport. Fortunately, I learned that some missionaries kept private landing strips. One immediate hurdle that Bob and I had to cross was Sam's refusal to do anything illegal. He was particularly stubborn on this point and is much larger and stronger than me or Bob. Luckily, he is also trusting, and he doesn't read Indonesian. One official had already offered to give us a *Surat Jalan* to fly to Wamena, the only Dani village where military protection could be assured. Wamena was several hundred miles from where we wanted to go, but the official said that there was a mountain nearby. After giving him a bribe of $50, he gave me the *Surat Jalan* to Wamena: I showed it to Sam and told him we had permission to go to Carstensz Pyramid. Next Bob and I had to find a bush pilot willing to fly us there.

Our savior came in the form of Leroy Kelm, a solidly built man with silver muttonchop sideburns who flies for the Missionary Air Fellowship and Seventh-Day Adventists. Since there are no roads in Irian Jaya, except in the vicinity of Jayapura, Leroy brings supplies to jungle villages and missionaries, flying daily over uncharted territory and visiting Stone Age cultures. At night he returns to his tidy home with his own landing strip, hangar, and manicured garden, and to his wife and daughter. Leroy was intrigued by our plans and agreed to fly us as near to Carstensz Pyramid as possible. He regretted that we couldn't land at the Dani village of Ilaga, ten days' walk from the mountain. "All I have left is my Aero Commander," he explained. "I had a small Cessna I could have gotten in there, but I crashed it in the jungle a couple of months ago. The closest I can get with the bigger plane is Mulia, a couple of days farther out from Ilaga." We said that would be fine, but then he added, "The folks in Ilaga are at war with Mulia because of a few women and pigs that were stolen in a raid last month."

Realizing that it was our only option, we decided to go for it. Taking off at dawn, we were happy to find clear skies and spectacular views of the rugged jungle landscape. There were occasional clearings with grass huts, called *awis*, which looked like fat haystacks sunk in deep valleys. Leroy agreed to fly us over Carstensz Pyramid for an aerial view and to locate the path we would follow to reach it. We flew over a small cluster of huts which, he told us, was Mulia, and passed Ilaga a few minutes later. Leroy again lamented crashing his other plane, reiterating the problem of walking from Mulia. After we had circled the peak, he said, "Aw, what the heck, I'll try to put her down in that potato patch," pointing to a tiny clearing on a hillside above Ilaga. "I sure do wish I hadn't crashed the Cessna," he repeated, while he sent the Aero Commander into a steep dive. My terror mounted as Leroy began muttering the Lord's Prayer under his breath as we neared a muddy field.

We touched down neatly enough, but the look on Leroy's face told us that something was seriously wrong. The plane did not slow down, but instead skidded on the mud as if it were an icy highway.

We slid a couple hundred feet, with the drop at the end of the clearing looming larger and closer at an alarming rate. Then we veered toward an embankment, sliding diagonally until the tires started sinking in the mud. The plane spun violently to a halt, the left wingtip a mere fifteen feet from a drop-off into dense jungle.

I was still shaking like a leaf in a tornado when, twenty minutes later, Leroy turned the plane and prepared to say good-bye. "I can't believe you are going to trek from here and try to climb that mountain wall," he said. "That is absolutely the craziest thing I have ever heard of! Actually, I take that back—when I was home visiting my sister last year I saw some guys on television jump from a bridge, attached to long rubber bands. That was the craziest thing I've ever seen! But this is close."

Bob told him that I was the man he had seen bungee jumping on television. Without batting an eye Leroy said, "That figures," and left us to our adventure.

Learning the Limits

To have a great adventure, and survive, requires good judgment. Good judgment comes from experience. Experience, of course, is the result of poor judgment. I finished high school in Illinois as a romantic dreamer in search of a quest. Like many teenagers, I had the ability to focus intensely on the present, maximizing the moment, with little thought for long-term consequences. I headed for college thinking that I would devote my energies to the noble art of healing. However, I spent the first three months of my freshman year exploring the social opportunities, learning about my classmates, playing tennis, and searching for a romantic calling. Then, reality hit. Exams approached and I hadn't opened a book in weeks.

I sat in the library, depressed and too overwhelmed to even start my work, when I saw a title on a bookshelf in front of me, *True Mountain Disaster Stories*. I began to read. After a couple of hours of learning about people freezing to death in crevasses, crawling off mountains with broken legs, and watching their friends swallowed by avalanches, I felt better. My problems were relatively minor. I focused on my work and got it done. From then on, whenever I felt down, I'd drift over to the Michael Ellenwood Curtis collection of mountaineering literature at the Yale Cross Campus Library. My habit grew to four hours a day as I became fascinated with mountaineering and adventure. Mountaineering became a romantic ideal for me. The pure, simple quest of man against nature and the struggle to ascertain one's own limits seemed a worthy goal. My reading also enthralled me with the variety of cultures, religions, and environments on our planet. I dreamed of the Alps, Africa, Antarctica, South America, and the Himalayas. H. W. Tilman, Heinrich Harrer, and Sir Richard Francis Burton became my heroes.

I finished my freshman year playing number one on the Yale varsity tennis team and contemplated playing on the pro tour. That summer I went to Europe with my doubles partner from junior tennis, Chuck Meurisse, to play the satellite tennis circuit. I lost consistently and watched the struggles of players, much better than I was, languishing on the minor league tour. After losing in the qualifying round for the Swiss Grand Prix tournament in St. Moritz I noticed a sign advertising a "Climbing Week," celebrating the centenary of the Swiss Mountain Guides' association. I went to the Guides' office where I used my German-English dictionary to discern that they had "very strenuous," "strenuous," and "not so strenuous" tours available. I read the lists of the mountains and routes each group would climb. Unfortunately, I couldn't resist showing off my knowledge of the history of mountaineering in the Alps, and asked, "Will the climb of the North Face of Piz Palu be via the Bonnati route?" The man said "Ja!" clearly excited to see that I knew the route. He promptly signed me up for the "most strenuous" tour.

No one else in my group of eight clients and four guides spoke English. The first day we hiked for eight hours up to a hut. During dinner the head guide gave a short speech in German. After the meal the rest of my group went to sleep. I was optimistic as I clearly was not as tired from the day's walk as they were. It was only six o'clock in the evening and I was wired on excitement and nervousness. At around eleven o'clock I tried to get some sleep. In the alpine huts everyone sleeps together on long mattresses. This hut was crowded and it was impossible to lie down without bumping up against your neighbor. In addition, lots of people were snoring loudly and many had been in the mountains for several weeks without bathing and the hut had a very ripe aroma. I lay awake until about half of the people got up at around midnight. I spread out and quickly fell asleep. The next thing I knew, a flashlight was shining in my face. Three angry people were swearing at me in German. My watch said it was two o'clock. Everyone else in my group had his back-pack on and was ready to go. I struggled with my things in the dark and finally staggered out into the cold, starry night forty minutes later.

We walked uphill for a few hours until we reached the base of a glacier. Everyone quickly put on his crampons. Not only did I not know how to put on crampons, but I had not adjusted my pair to fit my boots. The guide fumbled with wrenches to adjust them in the dark while everyone began to get cold. A similar, but shorter fiasco occurred when it was time to tie into the rope. I was handed the middle of the rope and stared at it, dumbly, until the guide came over and tressed me up while muttering under his breath. By first light we were climbing an ice slope and it began to snow lightly. I became increasingly more nervous as the angle steepened. My calves began to burn and I started to get out of breath. Finally, the slope eased and we pulled onto a flat area just as the storm increased into a blizzard.

"This must be the summit," I thought. I was thrilled to have climbed my first mountain and relieved that I would be able to do the climbing on this tour. Gleefully, I took out my instamatic camera for a summit shot. I handed the camera to the man next to me, smiled broadly, and motioned for him to take my picture. "Sheistmeister mensch!" he said turning away with a look of disgust. No one else in the group seemed very happy either. Oh well. "They must be mad because the storm obscures the view," I thought. We ate a little chocolate and bread and started down, descending to a different hut. (Mountaineering huts are positioned in key places throughout the Alps and are used by anyone needing shelter or a rest.)

In this hut I met a man who spoke English. From him I learned that my group had not even attempted our proposed climb. We had hiked near the base, but because of me, we arrived too late to make the ascent. I had earned the affectionate nicknames of "Dumsheist," or "Sheistmeister mensch," from my companions. The storm kept me hut-bound with eleven people who hated me for the next three days. My interpreter asked me about my climbs in America and wondered how I had gotten onto the "expert" course with no experience. I told him that I thought that I had signed up for the "strenuous tour." He laughed in amazement, and then explained the mistake to my guides. Three were in favor of sending me down. The youngest guide, Sepp, found my situation amusing and indicated that I should climb with him alone. I contemplated my options. I was in the mountains and had a guide willing to take me. I decided to follow the road to its conclusion. When the weather cleared my terror gave way to increasing enthusiasm as Sepp hauled me up the next three climbs to complete the tour.

I returned to Yale for my sophomore year with a short memory for the bad moments. I was happy to have made a few summits and survived and had no plans to climb ever again. Then, at a party, I heard an attractive woman talking about hiking in the Alps. She fit another of my romantic ideals and, in an effort to meet her, I casually mentioned that I'd done some mountain climbing in the Alps. She was not impressed and walked away, leaving me face to face with a fanatic. His eyes were fully dilated, his veiny forearms bulged, and talk of climbing brought out a manic grin. Henry Lester was gesticulating in the air about routes in the Shawangunks. He was excited to hear about my climbs. The next thing I knew, Henry decided that we had to go rock climbing together, tonight! We drove to the Shawangunk Mountains in the Catskill region of New York, the mecca of rock climbing on the East Coast. Henry soon found out that I was totally clueless. He was shocked to see me take out my hiking boots. It became clear that there were two choices: either Henry would beat the shit out of me and leave me on the side of the road, or I would buy a pair of rock climbing shoes and endeavor to have Henry teach me to climb.

Henry taught me how to tie into the rope and belay my partner for safety. He then led up an overhanging face as if he were dancing up the stairs. I was unable to find any holds. I followed with a lot of help from the rope. Henry was a patient teacher. After one weekend I was enthralled with rock climbing: It is a combination of chess, vertical ballet, and gymnastics. You have to mentally figure out how to use the array of holds the mountain offers you, then perform the moves, which involve a harmony of strength, balance, and weight transfer. Climbing demands a total focus of the mind and body onto the moment: You are a being, stuck to a wall, where the entire universe boils down to reaching the next hold. There is no future or past, only now. Once I was able to climb a route of one difficulty, Henry moved things up a level so that I was always struggling at my limit. Henry trained like a maniac. I fell under his influence. I did pull-ups on small edges, traversed a rock wall climbing sideways until my forearms cramped. I eventually built up to the point where I mentally willed my fingers to hang on for a half hour after the cramps began. I went to Ragged Mountain, a small nearby crag, and set up top ropes to safely practice at my limit most afternoons. When winter came, Henry and I went to New Hampshire to climb frozen waterfalls.

In my senior year, Yale nominated me for the Rhodes Scholarship and Marshall Scholarship competitions, which provide two years of funded study in England. The criteria for selection was outlined in Cecil Rhodes' will as "citizenship, leadership, academic aptitude and love of vigorous life." The Marshall fund was endowed by the British government as a thank you for the Marshall Plan after World War II and effectively doubled the number of awards. I was awarded a Marshall Scholarship to study philosophy at Oxford University and deferred medical school. With my next two years fully funded I was able to spend the summer after graduation doing nothing but climbing. I started in Yosemite Valley and hit most of the classic Western rock climbing areas. I also climbed a few mountain routes in Colorado and Wyoming. By the time I left for England I was leading routes just below the top level in American rock climbing and had survived most of the stupid mistakes a beginner can make in the mountains.

During my first day at University College, Oxford, I heard an American voice say, "Doug, I've got my car all packed and my climbing gear organized, are you sure you don't know anyone who rock climbs?" I sauntered over and introduced myself to Bob Shapiro. Twenty minutes later we were off for the sea cliffs of Cornwall. Bob turned out to be an ideal partner. He had read many of the same romantic adventure books, and is more than simply a dreamer—he is a doer. We followed a book called *Hard Rock* that describes the most famous climbs in Britain, ticking off the classics. To this point all of the climbs I had done were listed in guide books. I knew their difficulty and I knew what I was getting myself into. Bob convinced me that real adventure involves going places where you don't know what you might encounter. For our first long vacation Bob tried hard to get me to hitchhike with him from England to the West Coast of Africa, with stops to climb desert spires in the Sahara and to ride camels with the Bedouin. I turned him down to go on a trip to Thailand, Malaysia, and Indonesia with Ed Hundert, the smartest person I've ever met, and Jerry Howe, an ex-football player, whose quiet craziness fed off my enthusiasms. The combination of our personalities and talents pushed the three of us into an exploration of ourselves and an expansion of our minds through the seamy underbelly of Southeast Asia.

Returning to Oxford for our second year, Bob and I renewed our climbing with a passion in both England and the Alps. Bob also found several indigenous trust funds that are remnants of the days when it was considered a sacred duty of Oxford gentlemen to go off and civilize people around the world. The vice master of our college was David Cox, a former president of the Alpine Club. He steered us to the "A. C. Irvine Grant for Oxford gentlemen to explore strenuous holidays in mountains abroad." Professor Cox explained to us that the more exotic locale we picked, the more money we would get.

Two of my favorite books from my Yale reading days were *White Nile* by Alan Moorehead, about the exploration of central Africa and the search for the source of the Nile (which led to the discovery of the Mountains of the Moon) and H. W. Tilman's *Snow on the Equator*; I particularly enjoyed his account of his climbs in the Ruwenzori Range. Bob and I received an A. C. Irvine Grant to go to Uganda to do technical climbing in the Ruwenzori. Unfortunately, political problems arose. The civil war which led to the fall of Idi Amin broke out a month before our departure. Bob, who had already spent time in African jails after illegally entering Benin on the national holiday celebrating the slaughter and ouster of all white people from Benin, thought it might still be safe in the mountains. However, the U.S. State Department said, "Absolutely not! The remnants of Amin's troops are in the foothills of the Ruwenzori." So, at the last minute, we changed our sights to go to Tanzania, climb Mount Kilimanjaro, and then on to Kenya to do a technical ascent on Mount Kenya. However, the day before our departure the border between Tanzania and Kenya closed, and we opted to just go to Kenya. I knew that Mount Kenya was a huge mountain with no easy way to the top. Our goals were modest. We hoped to just get to the top of the mountain. We ended up making the first ascent of the hardest rock climb on Mount Kenya. This was a trip that changed my climbing focus and expanded my horizons into the realm of true adventure.

"Dayenu"—Mind Expansion on Mount Kenya

DAYENU IS A HEBREW WORD which translates to "it would have been enough" and was important to Moses, the first great Jewish alpinist, in his discussions with God. Dayenu is also relevant to me, and to Bob Shapiro, a modern Jewish alpinist with whom I had the pleasure of climbing on Mount Kenya during December and January of 1980.

We intended to do the normal route and hoped to try a few of Mount Kenya's classics. I would have settled for the normal route only. It was my first journey to a big mountain and just being there would have been enough. And, even if I failed to acclimatize and could not get up anything, we still would be seeing a bit of Africa. *Dayenu.*

We flew via Cairo, and opted for a stopover. Checking our equipment at the airport, we ventured into three of the most action-packed, outlandish days and nights imaginable. The details are not important. Suffice it to say that it was A-5 living, the Great Pyramid was ascended, and, in a region known as "The Mountain," a man named Mohammed got us acclimatized to an altitude higher than Messner will ever know (without oxygen). What the hell were we going to Kenya for? *Dayenu.*

Our descent from the heights of Cairo proved to be an epic. African airlines strictly enforce a twenty-kilo-per-man weight limit. To our horror, we discovered that it would cost $200 to get our equipment to Nairobi, which was more cash than we had. We hastily ducked out of the check-in line and retreated to a deserted corner of the airport to regroup. The strategy was clear: cut down on apparent weight. We emptied the haul sac on the ground and dressed ourselves in long underwear, wool pants, gaiters, mountain boots, wool sweaters and of course, our ceremonial necklace of Chouinard stoppers and hexes (part of Bob's religion). And of course, we would not feel safe without hard hats on; this was, after all, 1980, and we were flying on a Boeing 727, which is a jet, like a DC 10. (There had already been two crashes that year.) Finally, we crammed the rest of our heavy hardware into carry-on luggage.

Confident of shedding the required weight and as inconspicuous as a Ubangi warrior in Phoenix, Arizona, we returned to the check-in counter. The Egyptians may never have seen climbing equipment, but they did recognize a financial opportunity. The supervisor came over and said that he admired our sense of adventure, while asking for a bit of *backsheesh*. Sweating profusely from the heat, we happily paid the $5 bribe and were off to Kenya.

East Africa is a tourist paradise. We spent our first eight days on a superb photographic safari. In the game parks we got to know John Rutt, an American climber who also hoped to climb on Mount Kenya but did not have a partner. John had climbed at Hell's Gate Forge with Vince Fayad, one of the best local climbers. The three of us visited Vince at the Mountain Club of Kenya before heading to the mountain. He was extremely helpful, telling us all the routes that were in condition and giving us recommendations. Vince also cautioned us not to be too confident because due to weather and altitude, only a small percentage of competent climbers reach the summit and even fewer do more than one route.

The next day John, Bob, and I arrived in Naro Moro, where the approach to the mountain starts. This is also where the logistical hassles begin. It is possible to go by car for twenty-eight kilometers up a dirt track to the Met Station at ten thousand feet. Unfortunately, the Naro Moro River Lodge has a monopoly on four-wheel-drive transportation and charges $70 for the forty-minute journey. We thus had to spend a full day trying to hitch a ride. The next problem was getting our things up the mountain. We had three weeks of food in addition to all of our climbing and camping gear. The porters charge higher rates in the Christmas season. Being on a low budget, we decided to make two carries each rather than pay for the porters. We divided our gear into three heavy and three light sacs and began hiking with the heavier ones.

The trail up Mount Kenya is phenomenally beautiful, passing through a bamboo forest, thick rain forest, and then into an area called the vertical bog. It is as unpleasant as the name implies. We trudged in constant drizzle and mud above the ankle for over an hour. This steep section finally gives way to the lovely Teleki Valley with giant groundsel and lobelia plants. As dusk approached, we arrived at the Teleki hut at 13,500 feet, where we spent Christmas Eve.

Our Christmas present was a spectacular view of the peaks and a three-hour slog to base camp. We pitched our tents in a beautiful meadow, bordered by a glacial stream, directly below Midget Peak at 14,500 feet. I had a bit of altitude sickness and all three of us were exhausted. After a short discussion of "What do you guys think about getting porters to bring up the rest of our gear?" "Definitely." "I'm for it," we reached the hard question of who would go to get them. Twenty minutes later, I walked down to the porters' shelter near Klarwill's hut at 13,650 feet and hired three men. We had to pay double rates because of Christmas but, lazing about all afternoon and evening, we gloated that we were paying ourselves three dollars an hour to take it easy. A real bargain.

In the morning we felt better and decided to attempt the normal route the following day. We hiked to Point Lenana at 16,355 feet which is the fourth highest peak and attainable with technical climbing. We descended to Top Hut, where we spent a restless night. At 5:00 A.M. we crossed the Lewis Glacier. As the first rays of sun warmed the rock, John, Bob, and I tied into our ropes and began to climb the "normal route." The guidebook time is four and a half hours to the summit of Nelion and our 6:00 A.M. start placed us there just before five in the afternoon.

Unfortunately, we never got seriously off route, encountered bad weather, or suffered from the altitude, and thus were left without an excuse for our slow time.

We decided to spend the night in the four-man Lobonar shelter, a structure that Ian Howell made thirteen solo ascents of the mountain to build. After that much effort, we felt obliged to stay. Also, our tired bodies were not fit for the descent even if we had time for it. Lastly, we stayed on Nelion, in hopes of crossing over to Batian, the higher of Mount Kenya's twin summits, in the morning. Expecting to be able to descend the same day, we had not brought any extra clothing or food, and the twelve hours of darkness seemed interminable. Rising directly on the equator, the sunlight temperature on Mount Kenya is very warm. However, at night you realize that you are above seventeen thousand feet, as the temperature is well below freezing. Searching for extra padding to stuff down our clothes for insulation, we discovered a hut register and read about Ian Allen and Ian Howell doing the first ascent of Equator, a very hard line on the Diamond Buttress, the day before. Shivering and rubbing our feet with tired hands, we wondered what kind of supermen could climb that hard at this altitude.

In the morning our frozen bodies were greeted by swirling powder snow and a two inch blanket on the top. Batian was out of the question. With the first slowing of the storm at 11:00 A.M. we began the descent. By noon the sun was shining brightly. The horrors we feared never came about. Back at camp we gorged ourselves to celebrate the first big mountain ascent made by John and me. *Dayenu.*

As the sun went down, we watched a waterfall flowing down the Diamond Couloir and realized that if we wanted to try an ice route we would have to go soon. The next morning Bob and I departed camp at 5:00 A.M. to attempt the classic Ice-Window Route. It follows a hidden gully just right of the Diamond Couloir. The paths merge at the top of the Chouinard-Covington headwall. The Window is not as desperate as its neighbor, averaging fifty-five degree mixed rock and ice climbing with only one short vertical section on its thousand-foot length. Ideal ice conditions on this side of the mountain are in the July to October season and we encountered soft-fading ice in places and verglassed rock for three hundred feet.

Enjoyable climbing led us into the spectacular ice cave that gives the route its name. We entered a vast cavern guarded by sixty-foot icicles, climbed to the back and chopped a window out of the other side. Being the first party on the route since September, we had to hack through three feet of solid blue ice. The exposure is incredible as one wriggles out of the window to stand near the top of the Diamond Couloir's headwall with 180 feet of vertical ice beneath. Happily it soon leans back to the comfortable sixty degrees of the Diamond Glacier which leads to the Gate of the Mists.

Not wishing to endure another uncomfortable night out, we carried food, a stove, extra clothing, and sleeping bags on the climb. The heavy packs slowed us down and we again reached the summit just before dark, prepared for the bivouac. We were not, however, prepared for the company. This we found aplenty in the shelter. Four Italians who spoke no English smiled at us as we pushed the aluminum door open. We spent a warm but contorted night. The next morning the sun shone brightly and we crossed over to Batian for photographs on the highest summit of Mount Kenya.

Back at camp we celebrated the classic ascent with cold Jello crystals and straight glucolin as our MSR stoves refused to work with the fuel we bought in Kenya. The next day, while festering in the sun, we decided that two summit climbs were enough. We would do a rock route on Point John and one on Midget Peak and then head down to the outcrops where we belonged. The next afternoon Bob and I climbed the easy South East Gully to the top of Point John. On the way back to camp Bob noticed a beautiful slab that seemed to lead nowhere. Just our type of climb.

At noon the next day I began the first pitch with John belaying and Bob taking photographs of our first, first ascent. The climbing was delicate, but on balance, gradually steepening from seventy-five degrees to near vertical at the stance 150 feet up. I considered abseiling off, but the dihedral above looked like it might go and I only had a single rope. Thus, I brought Bob up and set out on the next pitch. It was difficult, with loose rock, and I laced it with runners. The excitement of whether the route would go, combined with the increase in commitment added an element I had never before experienced in climbing.

After 150 feet I arrived at a stance and pondered the alternatives. It looked feasible to move up and right into an easy gully but then the route would lead nowhere, giving a hard four-hundred-foot start to an easy gully climb. The other choice was to move left on nearly nonexistent holds and try to gain an overhanging crack that might lead to the South Ridge. I asked Bob if he wanted to lead. He generously said that since this was my first, first ascent I could do all the leading. Thanks a lot.

I went up twenty feet and placed a thumbnail sized metal wedge into a crack, clipped the rope to it and decided to try to reach the overhanging crack. I could see two very thin holds and, rechecking my "protection," moved left. I told Bob to watch me and that after I fell I would pendulum to the crack. More microedges, the size of the edge of a quarter, materialized, and twenty-five feet later my nervous body reached the crack, where I happily slotted a "Friend," a self-camming anchor, and moved up on good jams to a hanging belay. The next pitch followed the crack for a few feet and then moved left again on a vertical face with large incut holds for the full 165-foot length of my rope to a nice roomy ledge. Bob and I were ecstatic. After one short enjoyable pitch we joined the classic Grade IV South Ridge.

The Tabin-Shapiro direct start provided us with a strong feeling of creative accomplishment. Moreover, we came to the happy realization that ordinary mortals can safely do serious technical climbing at altitude. *Dayenu.*

Back in camp we were racing with adrenaline and our natural high lasted all night. The next day Bob opted for a rest and John and I decided to do an afternoon ascent of Midget Peak. Approaching the gully between Point John and Midget, I noticed a possible line leading up and right and suggested that we give it a try. We checked the guidebook to make certain that

it was not there, and set off. The second pitch went back slightly
left, and after five long pitches we were on the summit. The
climbing was not overly hard. Nor was the climbing overly
pleasant, with sharp, prickly lichen cutting our fingers on many
holds and some loose rock. However, the same thrill of adventure made the route worthwhile.

Climbing technically difficult rock following a guidebook
never gave this sense of accomplishment. In two days my climbing horizons had been broadened from a rock gymnastics
approach to an understanding of the thrills of commitment and
the unknown which a big mountain can provide. Our trip to
Mount Kenya was successful in mental as well as physical
accomplishments. *Dayenu.*

Back at camp I encountered one stoked Bob Shapiro. He had
been receiving propaganda all day from Vince Fayad, who was
now camped directly below us. Vince had done the second
ascent of the Diamond Buttress Original Route with Ian Allen
and described it as the best hard rock route on the mountain. In
addition to the route's quality, he convinced Bob that doing the
fourth ascent would be a great way to end an already successful
climbing holiday. Knowing that I was on a first ascent kick, Bob
quickly pointed out that ours would be the first all American
and first Jewish rope on the Diamond Buttress. Enough said.

We set out to do the type of climb that one week before we
had believed was only accessible to a strange breed of superhuman high-altitude hardmen. The psychological barriers were
broken down. A solid week of sunshine put the rock in perfect
condition for free climbing. The first two pitches yielded interesting and sustained difficult rock climbing. Surprisingly we felt
as comfortable as if we were at sea level, and our confidence
grew. On the third pitch I encountered a fixed piton, clipped the
rope into it and turned a six-foot overhang with large incut
holds. When Bob joined me at the belay he said that I had just
freed the aid overhang. "Bullshit," I said. Bob, who had been
given the route description by Vince, was certain it was the aid
overhang and decided we should try to free the entire route. I
was dubious as a massive roof loomed a few hundred feet higher.

Two pitches later I found myself 130 feet above Bob with nowhere to go. I was hanging from a single finger wedged in a crack just above a fixed piton and I could see no useful holds above me. After ten minutes my arms were pumped and my mind was gripping up. Finally, I downclimbed twenty-five feet and brought Bob up. "You better lead this crack, I can't do it," I muttered. Bob claimed that this was the tension traverse and it was time to move right. "Bullshit," I said. Bob was insistent. I protested that we were getting off route, believing that we hadn't even reached the aid overhang.

Bob led off, ending all discussion. After clipping the rope into a piton, he moved right on fingernail edges and reached the next dihedral without coming off. He gave a whoop of joy. "We freed the tension traverse," he happily yelled back, adding "very thin stuff." "Bullshit," I said. "It was thin," Bob insisted. "I believe that, but I don't think this is the route," I yelled.

By now the rope was tugging at me and I had no choice but to follow. I was not convinced we were on route until we reached the "three star" bivy ledge that I had heard Vince describe. I gave out a whoop and yelled "Bob, we freed the Diamond Buttress."

Over dinner we happily discussed the day's accomplishments. According to Vince, we were above the four hardest pitches and all of the aid. All of the previous parties had spent two nights on the face. We decided that if we dropped our extra hardware and bivy gear down the Diamond Couloir, we could get up and off the same day. After a spectacular starry night Bob brought his very full pack to the couloir, and we watched our extra gear fall and land on the glacier below. This done, we set off with only one light load which the second carried.

At noon we began to regret our decision, finding ourselves still far below the summit. The second day's climbing was sustained and hard with a less-obvious line to follow. We got slightly off route and had to turn a strenuous overhang and climb two energy-sapping steep cracks, all above 16,500 feet. When we finally reached the easy summit ridge it was after 4:00 P.M. We still had four easy full-rope-length runouts to the summit of

Batian, the descent into the Gate of the Mists, and the climb back up to Nelion, before starting the descent. We arrived on Nelion, exhausted, shortly after five. With only cagoules to go over our sweaters, we were not eager to spend the night and immediately headed down. This was our third descent, and knowing exactly where to find the abseils, we reached the Lewis Glacier just before dark.

It was not the first ascents or the freeing of the buttress that were most meaningful, but the psychological breakthrough that we made. We discovered that after fifteen days of climbing above fourteen thousand feet we could acclimatize like the mythical supermen. We gained the confidence to extend ourselves on a big mountain in a remote setting. We realized that the most difficult obstacles to surmount in climbing, as in life, are mental. All this, and all we had dreamed of was making it to the summit of Mount Kenya. *Dayenu!*

The World's Most Daring Sportsman

In 1933, H. W. Tilman decided he'd like to check out the beach at Cameroon. Only problem was, at that moment Tilman happened to be at his beach-front home in Mombassa, about three thousand miles away. To reach Cameroon's sandy shore required the first east-to-west traverse of Africa through the dense, uncharted jungles of Uganda and the Congo. Tilman was undeterred. Alone on his bicycle, armed only with a machete, he rode off into the sunset, probably pausing each afternoon at four for tea. A little more than two months later, he reached his destination. At the age of fifty-six, with almost twenty-five years of exploration in Africa and the Himalayas behind him, the irrepressible old codger then bought a boat and, over several expeditions, eventually sailed it around the world. He even made a trip to the South Pole, which he reached just before is sixty-ninth birthday.

The decline of the British Empire and an increasingly well-charted globe have made the Tilmans of this world a dying breed. Once, an Oxford education, tweed trousers, two pairs of socks, and a heavy coat were all a British gentleman explorer needed to make an all-out assault on the summit of Mount Everest. These days it seems to require a six-figure budget, international sponsorship, and a small army of Sherpas to get that far. Indeed, "the right stuff" is in distressingly short supply. Or seems to be, anyway, until you cast your eye toward one David Kirke and that cradle of the eccentric idle rich, the university town of Oxford, England.

Kirke does not look like an adventurer or a hero of any kind. In fact, seen in his army-surplus coat (secured with safety pins) after a typical Friday evening at a smoky Oxford pub called "The Bear," he looks as though he might need help walking home. With a slight beer drinker's paunch, bristling gray-flecked beard topped by bulging eyes and receding brown curls, he seems the quintessential upper-class twit gone to seed. Which he is. But he also happens to be the roguish kingpin of the world's only club devoted exclusively to those sports and diversions so dangerous, so improbable, so utterly outlandish that no one else would even think of them, let alone try them. As founder, director, idea man, and prime mover of the Oxford Dangerous Sports Club, Kirke is out to prove that the call of the wild still comes through loud and clear. He continually demonstrates that neither skill nor experience are needed to set a hang-gliding record, fly an airplane, climb a mountain, scale a live volcano, or leap from a high-speed train. As Kirke carries his celebration of the dilettante to manic extremes, his actions tend to confirm what his friends cheerfully admit: he is, by all standards, deranged.

Even in his upbringing, the thirty-four-year-old Kirke seems to have been molded as a Victorian adventurer. With an education in self-reliance through his early years, Kirke proceeded, well prepared, to Oxford. He spent three undistinguished years there, as befits a man of good taste, leaving with a "gentleman's third" in English literature to take up journalism in London. Whatever the initial romance of a profession that involved watching other people do exciting things, Kirke found early on that he much preferred being watched himself. Helped by the fact that no one seemed to think he was destined to be a great journalist, Kirke packed his bags in 1970 and returned to Oxford.

There, with Christopher Baker and Ed Hulton, two friends who share a bit of that wild gleam that lights Kirke's eyes, he set about experimenting with adventure. Where some Oxonians become self-taught experts in dead languages or Australian wines, he would make himself the world expert on what he calls life-questioning sport.

The first step was to sample the traditional dangerous sports. During the summer of 1977, with no expertise and little equipment, Kirke clambered to the top of the Matterhorn. That August, without ceremony or training, he and Baker launched themselves down the Landquart in Switzerland, thus becoming the greenest of novices ever to survive what is probably Europe's most treacherous stretch of white water.

The reckless successes began piling up as Kirke, fired by his growing enthusiasm for danger, looked for ever greater potential disasters. Later that summer, though he lacked a pilot's license, he somehow rented a small airplane, which he managed to get airborne and return safely to earth without ever having flown one of the contraptions before.

The birth of the Oxford Dangerous Sports Club, however, was delayed until October, when Kirke planned his first group activity: champagne brunch for six, followed by a jump from Rockall, a sixty-three-foot sea stack off the coast of Scotland. After a climb that was treacherous in itself, Kirke's little party looked down to where the ebb and flow of crashing waves created a cycle of filling and emptying pools—one instant safely full, the next nothing but bare rock for a diver to land on. Deciding that discretion was, indeed, the better part of valor, several would-be members of Kirke's new club turned around and risked the climb back down. Two people finally jumped, and Kirke himself dived headfirst into the freezing water, though he had never even jumped from a high board before. All that finally marred this true baptism of the club was that the boys already knew how to swim.

The following summer, for Kirke and his club, was devoted to experimentation. Having by then tried all traditional dangerous sports of importance, they felt it was time to move on, to invent new ones. In addition to the simple thrill that novelty provided—and it was becoming increasingly hard to thrill Kirke—there was an increased element of risk involved. Danger was relatively easy to evaluate when one knew what had happened before; it assumed mysterious dimensions, however, when the odds were unknown. It was at about that time that the calculations for all the group's events—the crucial calculations of speed, velocity, impact, and so forth that determined survivability—were turned over to Simon Keeling and Alan Weston, two of Kirke's buddies who had taken their respective Oxford degrees in engineering and computing, and who thus could be counted on to produce reasonably reliable estimates. However, because the dangerous sportsmen were not about to let the tedious certitude of modern science interfere with the spirit of their challenge to nature, they adhered to a policy of undertaking only adventures never before attempted, so that there would always be an element of uncertainty involved.

Thus did various bobsled runs in France and Switzerland take on new dimensions in the summer of 1979, when negotiated atop a block of ice fitted with a seat. Wheelchairs turned nearly lethal as they were moved out of hospital corridors and onto steep hillsides for the purpose of quick descent. During the traditional running of the bulls through the narrow Spanish streets of Pamplona, Kirke and company substituted skateboards for foot speed. And in what was planned as the climax of the summer, the tuxedo-clad sportsmen were to have parachuted into the Longleat animal park's lion enclosure, each armed with a revolver containing only one bullet. The fact that this event never came off probably had more to do with lack of organization than with lack of nerve.

Exactly what makes Kirke tread the edge of the great abyss with such regularity is impossible to say for sure. When he is not risking a final farewell, his daily schedule borders on the unbearably routine—a sort of burlesque of life in Oxford. Emerging every day about noon from his chaotic apartment, where books are strewn all over and trophies of dangerous ventures litter the shelves, he ambles to the center of town in time for lunch at The Bear. There, surrounded by his cronies, the world's most daring sportsman sits eating omelets and drinking pints of beer until the sun goes down. Then it's off to his club, where he can sit in a leather wing chair and read the papers with England's finest, warmed by frequent doses of good Scotch.

Now, admittedly, this is not the regimen of either genius or fitness. And, indeed, Kirke takes unconcealed pride in the fact that he is usually at least five years the senior of his fellow Dangerous Sports Club members and apparently in the worst shape of all. He also takes pride in the fact that while climbing Kilimanjaro, he went straight to the nineteen thousand-foot summit without missing a stride, while his young companions wheezed and gasped their way up behind him.

The secret of his stamina and of his remarkable ability to survive the unsurvivable is neither training nor any particular talent, but a psychological toughness that produces unparalleled performances through the sheer force of his will. Kirke assumes he will survive and, believing it, he does. With heroes of the era of the amateur—with men like Scott in the Antarctic and Stanley in Africa—he shares a mental determination that enables him to endure horrendous pain and to think clearly in the most disconcerting of crises. "Everyone has a certain level of anxiety," he says. "I direct my anxiety into the events I attempt. The rest of my life is very calm."

Maybe so, but to the impartial observer, Kirke's behavior is not as calm as he claims. A man who prefers extremes in every aspect of life, Kirke replaces the disintegrating army coat and safety pins each evening with an equally battered black tie and tails. He throws a succession of extravagant parties that seem to keep him stylishly in the hole. It may ultimately be more accurate to say that Kirke's "events" are the safety valve for anxieties and preoccupations that are larger than life.

But whatever the cause, there can be no doubt that by the fall of 1978, the manic gleam in Kirke's eyes had inspired a full-fledged organization of dangerous sportsmen and assorted hangers-on. With the trio of Baker, Weston, and Keeling forming the core of the club around Kirke, the sportsmen were beginning to stir interest in wider circles. Since their personal resources were rapidly dwindling and their schemes growing exponentially more expensive, that was a very good thing. Late in 1978, they enlisted the support of an independent film-production company and the BBC for a hang-gliding expedition off

Mount Kilimanjaro. Kirke had never bothered to master the sport, of course, but his smooth talking and confident air convinced the men holding the purse strings that he was champion.

The expedition served to clinch Kirke's status as a legend among the *cognoscenti* and, at the same time, proved a disaster for the BBC. Loaded down with hang-gliding apparatus, supplies, and the obligatory formalwear, two of Kirke's companions abandoned the attempt during the tortuous ascent. Weston, the only experienced hang glider in the group, got to the top but crashed on take-off, destroying his glider and injuring his ankle. Keeling, meanwhile, managed a take-off, then bounced his wing tip off the mountainside, swooped upward and then screamed back toward earth in a nylon-and-metal-tubed power dive leftward. The BBC captured approximately twelve seconds of filmed flight, which depicted the Kirke posterior disappearing into surrounding clouds. But what was the end of a short film clip best forgotten by the BBC was only the beginning for Kirke. Once enveloped by clouds, he continued to fly through the mist without a compass or an altimeter, eventually coming in for a gentle landing on a coffee plantation twenty-five miles away.

The Kilimanjaro exploit proved to be a crucial watershed in the history of dangerous sports. With it came a greater cohesiveness of the group and, symbolic of that new clubbiness, an official club tie (a silver wheelchair on black background). It also established the club as a media darling—and, just as important, convinced the sportsmen that anything they did was a media event. Kirke continued to indulge a mania for secrecy about preparations for the group's events, but he was increasingly receptive to the idea of coverage once the events were underway, particularly if that meant money. And, finally, it was Kilimanjaro that first prompted him to speculate seriously about what was to become the club's most famous invention—a modern variation on an ancient puberty ritual that would be suitable for mass-media coverage.

I met Kirke around this time. Bob Shapiro and I had just returned from our successful climbing trip to Mount Kenya and we were fired up for more equatorial ice climbing adventures.

We had both read Heinrich Harrer's book *I Come From the Stone Age* about his exploration and climbs in the Carstensz Range of Irian Jaya, New Guinea. His encounters with the Stone Age Dani natives had me mesmerized, and I'd long dreamed of going there. The Indonesian Government had closed access to the region, however, and the plan was on indefinite hold. About this time, British climber Peter Boardman, who had just returned from Irian Jaya, gave a slide show about his trip. One look at his slide of the unclimbed two-thousand-foot rock wall on the North Face of Carstensz Pyramid was enough. Bob and I immediately began applying for grants.

A few evenings later we were at The Bear discussing the possible trip. David Kirke and Alan Weston, a classmate of mine in University College, sat at our table. "New Guinea?" Kirke asked, his interest piqued. "You must try vine jumping!"

He explained in detail a curious New Guinea rite of passage where boys tie springy vines to their ankles, then leap from high trees. They hurtle, head first, toward the ground until the vine snaps them to a mind-jolting halt inches from the forest floor.

"Only we'll need something better than vines," Kirke said, almost to himself. He had already forgotten our climbing trip and was busily planning the details of his next "event." We were soon joined by Simon Keeling and many pints of beer. Before dawn it was jointly decided that bungee cord would be the perfect modern urban vine and that bridges should substitute for platforms in tall trees.

The first jump, on April Fools' Day, 1979, was from one of England's highest suspension bridges, the 245-foot Clifton Bridge in Bristol. One end of the bungee was tied to the bridge, the other to an improvised harness designed by Keeling and Weston. With champagne toasts, Kirke, Weston, Keeling, and Tim Hunt—younger brother of champion race-car driver James Hunt—all stepped off. Like tuxedo-clad yo-yos, the dangerous sportsmen dropped the full length of their cords, stretched another 100 feet waterward, and bounced back up nearly 200 feet; then it was down and up and down again, in bounces of decreasing magnitude, until they hung, limp but ecstatic, 120 feet below the bridge. It was only after Weston had popped the cork on the celebratory champagne he'd carried along on the leap that the remaining members of the party hauled them back up to the bridge.

Arrested and photographed, the sportsmen had achieved both of their objectives: They had garnered national publicity, and all four jumpers were alive, which proved their new sport could be played. After another trial leap that October from the Golden Gate Bridge in San Francisco, Kirke decided they were ready for the big time.

What he had his eye on was nothing less than the world's highest suspension bridge. Like a toothpick slung across a funnel, the 1,260-foot Royal Gorge Bridge spans the Arkansas River just outside Canon City, Colorado. The gap, which is about 800 feet wide at the top, narrows to less than 60 feet at the base. Without even having seen the bridge, the sportsmen were eager to jump from it. Keeling and Weston got to work on their computations. After much deliberation, they announced that a bungee cord 415 feet long, with Kirke attached, could be expected to stretch at least that distance again; Kirke would be subjected to a deceleration force of five gs and would pass out on the rebound.

Kirke was intrigued. "This will require total control, mental and physical, and you won't know the result until you wake up. How excellent!" he exclaimed. "If you do everything correctly up to the point you pass out, then you'll survive, but if you don't—if you make a mistake—then you'll die not even feeling your own death." But even as they indulged in that kind of existential reflection, Kirke and friends lost no time wrapping up the publicity and the dollar side of the expedition.

Back in early 1980, "That's Incredible!" the now-notorious ABC show that specialized in video-taping self-inflicted mutilation for mass consumption, had a lot less to its discredit than it would. Kirke was convinced that anything called "That's Incredible!" simply had to need his kind of adventure. As it turned out, he was right.

Kirke and the producers agreed on an $18,000 fee to fill the club's coffers. Fill them, that is, so they could be emptied again. For, in the spirit of the club, Kirke ordained that every cent of the take would be spent on the jump itself and associated celebration.

The television company scheduled the filming for March 6, 1980, and requested three jumpers. Kirke decided to do it his way or not at all. He insisted on flying over as many of the club members as wanted to go, and most of them converged on London first for a preflight party. From Paris came Hunt and Hubert Gibbs, a shy young musician who was to be the jump's official pianist. From Ireland came ex-Oxonian Anthony Murphy and his wife, Sophia. Oxford yielded Murphy's brother Rob, Kirke, and me, rock climber extraordinaire. I was in charge of tying the bungee cords. Kirke and I had become good friends. We enjoyed living vicariously through each other's brand of adventure. Recently he had consulted me on harnesses and knot tying for his bungees.

On the morning of the scheduled departure, a mildly intoxicated David Kirke pounded on my door at three o'clock. "Geoff," he stated matter-of-factly, "do come along to America and have a bit of sport with us."

"Huh?" I muttered. "What time is it?"

"Nearly half three." Kirke replied. "Our flight to San Francisco leaves from Heathrow at ten."

"David, I can't. I have a tutorial at eleven o'clock this morning and exams coming up," I argued.

"Pitch it!" he demanded. "We quite need you to fix the harnesses and handle the safety angle. I will pick up all of your expenses. What do you say?"

I thought to myself for a moment. "Would I regret this more if I do it or if I don't do it?" An instant later, now fully awake, I said, "O.K. I'm with you."

David smiled his broad grin, "Excellent! See you at the airport in a few hours." He handed me a club tie, shook my hand, then vanished back into the parties of the night.

Finally, tired and drunk from their various preliminary cele-brations, the party converged on San Francisco five days before the scheduled jump. Weston was to meet up with the crew at the jump site, but Paul Foulon, Weston's stepbrother and the group's second American, drove down from Portland in his pickup—bringing with him the bungees used in the Golden Gate jump the year before.

"Every event may be my last," Kirke declared, before we set out for Colorado in a convoy comprising a white Cadillac con-vertible, two small trailers, and the pickup. "Festivity is required. If anything goes wrong, the party must celebrate life, not mourn death."

A parody of a motorcade, the Dangerous Sports Caravan weaved, skidded, and violated the law at an average of seventy miles per hour across the Great American West, white Cadillac in the lead, packed to the brim with silly looking weirdos in ties and tails. To the uninitiated, the convoy itself looked like dangerous sport: $1280 worth of liquor stowed in the trunk, all being pumped with indecent haste into the already saturated livers of Britain's sickest and strangest, who even in England could not be relied on to find the right side of the road.

No one slept, of course, for total party required total com-mitment. Besides, if the revelers tried to sleep, they might actu-ally pass out, and given the amount of alcohol diluting the blood of those Englishmen, it might be weeks before they would see daylight again. After eighteen hours of continuous merrymaking, the Dangerous Sports Club pulled into the truck stop in Ely, Nevada, at six o'clock in the morning. The boys tightened their bow ties and swaggered in. Forty-five truckers' jaws dropped into sedimented cups of coffee. Warily, the wait-ress approached. Kirke smiled his evil smile, while all eyes bulged expectantly. Anthony Murphy, part of the supporting cast, stepped diffidently forward. Dressed in a Royal Navy din-ner jacket with tails, he peered benevolently at the permanent-waved waitress. "Excuse me, but can you tell me, how *viscous* is your porridge?"

Later that day, as we crossed into Utah, a storm blew in, and how the Brits loved it! Windows rolled up, visibility zero, we fishtailed wildly down the invisible road—forty miles an hour on a skating rink you couldn't even see! This was danger fit for dangerous men, and they reveled in every bit of it. With public school voices jabbering at cocktail-party levels, the drunken caravan roared on into the dark, a meteor of the English upper class burning insanely across the snowdrifts of the American desert.

We arrived in Canon City, fourteen miles outside Royal Gorge, one day before the jump. Up to that point, the club had been a bit worried about how seriously "That's Incredible!" was going to take its sport. One look at producer Alan Landsburg's preparations and all were reassured. In addition to a dozen cameramen, a helicopter had been rented for some aerial shots. Eyeing the chopper wistfully, Kirke said, "There may be some tangible benefits from this television company, after all. Perhaps I could persuade them to let me have a go with their helicopter."

At the site, the boys took a look around—and down. Standing atop the wind-swept bridge, 1,053 feet above what looked like a pencil line of river, the club looked for the first time just the slightest bit pensive. It was a long way down.

No time for regrets now, thought Kirke, and he took the rest of the Brits off for early afternoon drinks among the natives of Canon City, while the two Americans on the team set to work tying on the cords that would be used in the next day's jump.

It was a tricky business. In previous jumps, Kirke had explained, to my horror, they had used seven-millimeter yachting rope and overhand knots to secure the bungee cord to the bridge. With that sort of knot tying, the jumpers would have about a 50 percent chance of dropping directly into the river below. So we spent eight hours constructing a line from two strands of seventeen-millimeter bungee cord, then tying the line into a carefully designed mountaineering-rope anchor that would secure the cords while preventing a fatal, frictive rub between the bungee cord and the bridge. Meanwhile, a piano was rented for Gibbs. It began to look as though the event would come off.

Everyone was "quite keen" to be the first off the bridge. Kirke decided to have five jumpers leap simultaneously, on cords spaced evenly along the bridge. Kirke, in the middle, would be on a 415-foot length. Weston and Hunt would flank him on 240-foot lengths, leaving the outside positions for the novices (Foulon and me) on 120-foot cords.

The biggest risk was Kirke's. Dangling at the end of one thousand feet of line, to within a few feet of the water, he would be subject to immensely widened pendulum swings. The slightest breeze from the wrong direction could blow him off course and slap him into a sheer granite face only thirty feet away at the base. "Strawberry jam spread on rock" was Weston's cheerful description of the probable result of an error in his calculations.

Another problem was the force of gravity, and, again, Kirke was to be most affected. Exactly how much force he would be exposed to if all went well, no one really knew. The Weston-Keeling estimate of five gs seemed plausible, but no one would have been surprised if they'd been off by 200 percent. Astronauts in their specially designed suits pass out with a force of ten gs. No one wanted to think what would happen if any of the jumpers was head-down when the g force built up.

All in all, this was unmistakably a Dangerous Sports Club presentation: No one knew to precisely what length the bungee cords would stretch on a jump from this height. Moreover, no one had really tried to find out. Not knowing, and not wanting to know, was what the club was all about.

Our celebration lasted until three the next morning. The jump was planned for eight A.M., in order to minimize the breezes that could turn Kirke into a pulp; but it wasn't until nine that the first of the club staggered in. We quickly set up a portable bar right next to the ambulance thoughtfully provided by "That's Incredible!" Missing members of the club were pulled from bed at eleven o'clock but still had to dress for the event.

Overhead, the copter blades chopped ominously, and a crowd started to gather. Five characters dressed as game-show M.C.s were about to fling themselves off the bridge. This promised to be better than a hanging.

At noon, Kirke finally arrived, had a drink, and was promptly approached by the bridge authorities. They wanted him to sign forms relieving them of all responsibility. His hand trembled as he took the pen. He had to steady himself before he signed. No one had ever seen Kirke shake before.

Looking down at the looped bungee cords dangling off the bridge and blowing gently in the wind, the sportsters were beginning to think quite seriously about getting hurt, and to think especially that if anyone were going to get hurt, it would very likely be Kirke. Hearing that Weston and Keeling had estimated that he would come within nine feet of the river, Kirke approached me and said, "Geoff, old man, I realize you have worked hard on the preparations, but is it still possible to extend my rope by four and a half feet? I'm quite keen to just touch the bottom before bouncing up." When it was pointed out to him that he was likely to be unconscious, he decided to reconcile himself to the nine-foot margin. That settled, the club members wanted to enjoy a few leisurely drinks before the jump, but everyone else seemed impatient. The television crew began to worry about whether or not the leap would take place at all. The ambulance crew fretted about the winds whipping up the canyon, which would throw the jumpers off course. And the tourists complained of the cold and began to call for the jumpers to hurry. Kirke was undaunted. Quieter than usual, he requested that his breakfast of eggs Benedict be lowered to him after he jumped. While Gibbs played appropriate bungee music on the piano, Kirke pondered how to keep the eggs warm on the descent.

Finally, after posing for a picture next to the ambulance, the group began to get ready. Beyond having a few more drinks, that involved my tying each of them into a full body harness and attaching it to the bungee cord. The club has a tradition of never checking its own knots, and only Foulon, who was wearing a cowboy hat with his tuxedo, was gauche enough to inspect his harness. Weston, dressed in a gray morning suit and club tie, seemed worried as he was secured to his bungee, calling for "More drink, please." He lit a large Havana cigar and puffed nervously while the others were readied. Next to be tied in was Hunt, who sported a black tux with tails and a gray top hat secured under his chin.

Now, only minutes before leaping into the unknown, Kirke was moving slowly. Weston impatiently cried out, "*Please* get to your rope, David. I can't wait much longer. I have to jump off soon."

Kirke nodded and solemnly walked to the long cord in the middle. "Have a good one, old boy," he called to Weston. As I tied him to his harness, he tried to light his pipe, but his hands shook too much to strike the match. Dressed in a black morning suit with tails, a black-velvet top hat, and the club tie, he allowed one of the cameramen to assist him with a light. He quickly got control of himself and joked that the harness was too tight. "I really must go on a diet!" he exclaimed. With Gibbs at the piano setting the mood, I finished Kirke's knots and headed for my own rope. It was almost three o'clock.

Walking from Kirke to my place at the side, I was struck by the reality of what I was about to do. Until that moment, I had been so absorbed in the partying and preparations that I had not really worried about my own jump. Suddenly, there was nothing more I could do for the others. Now it was my ass out on the line. The sounds of classical piano and helicopter blades were replaced in my ears by the pounding of my heart. I gave a final glance at my comrades, then I looked down.

Nearly eleven hundred feet below, the river looked like a thread. The canyon walls seemed only inches apart. I trusted the bungee cords and the knots I had tied. I was the only one using a safety line—a security measure that Kirke considered highly unethical. Rationally, I knew I would be safe; yet I was gradually enveloped by fear. I tried to calmly remind myself that I'd been subjected to more danger than this climbing vertical rock walls. Just as I began to regain control of my trembling body, I was interrupted by a cameraman who said, "Boy, aren't you afraid that there safety rope will wrap around your neck as you bounce up and hang you as you fall back down?"

I hadn't been, but suddenly I was. My testicles quickly receded into the safety of my body. My entire groin tightened. My mind raced incoherently. The others were already over the retaining fence. I clambered after them while my panicked brain screamed, "No!"

For a moment, we paused on the farthest supports. It was reassuring, at least, to see how much farther Kirke's cord hung down into space, blowing gently at the limit of my vision. All sound ceased. Time stood still. Kirke raised his hand, signaled "One. Two. Three," then stepped calmly into the air.

I pushed off and my mind immediately signaled, "Error!" Like a cartoon figure, I desperately tried to walk back to the bridge while hanging motionless in the air. Then I fell.

My mind stopped. My heart stopped. The only thing moving was my body, free-falling into the void. My life became calm as I came to a gentle stop four hundred feet down—only to be catapulted violently skyward. Accelerating upward, totally out of control, I was elated. The bungee had held. I slowed to a stop again, now fifty feet below the bridge. Regaining body control, I was able to turn and see the other jumpers. Foulon, at the far side, was at the same height I was. Far below, Weston was beginning his first upward bounce. Kirke was still falling, a dot disappearing in the abyss. I watched them all during my next descent, noting happily that no one had become strawberry jam. I thoroughly enjoyed my last few bounces, trying several somersaults as I rose and fell.

Soon we were all hanging like spiders, suspended between heaven and earth in a giant V. The television helicopter circled us and we waved to it and to one another, thumbs up all around. It was now only a matter of waiting to be hoisted back up. Soon Hunt, Foulon, Weston and I were safely on the bridge. Foulon appropriately described the feeling for the television audience as "incredible."

Meanwhile, Kirke's cord proved to be making it impossible to pull him up. For nearly three hours, he hung nine hundred feet below us, without so much as an overcoat to protect him from the cold. With wind whipping up the canyon and the temperature near freezing, we knew he was in considerable pain. The harness would be cutting off circulation to his legs. The medical crew began to worry. Finally, we found a way to bring him up by pulling the bungee with a tow truck. When he reached the bridge, Kirke's only concern was the whereabouts of his prized top hat and pipe, both of which had been lost in his struggle to remain upright.

Kirke described the jump for the television cameras, saying such an experience "definitely gives one heightened appreciation for life." Privately, he admitted a slight disappointment with the event. The Weston-Keeling estimates had been way off. He hadn't passed out and had stopped a good one hundred feet short of the water. "Quite the worst of it was, I didn't get a good bounce," he said. "My cords stretched and stopped. The shorter jumps were definitely better sport."

While the television crew disbanded, Gibbs and various of the sportsmen took turns jumping. And, as always, the party went on.

For most of them, the Dangerous Sports Club is only an occasional diversion, so this was a rare event, to be savored and prolonged. Only Kirke has made the club a way of life, moving from one event to the next. In 1981, he made the first motor-ized-hang-glider crossing of the English Channel, nonstop from London to Paris. Since the Frenchman Jean Marc Boivin surpassed Kirke's high-altitude hang-gliding mark, Kirke has been trying to talk his way onto an expedition to the peak of Mount Everest. "I shall hang-glide off Everest," he predicted, "even if I must charter a helicopter to the summit." He is also planning "an extremely festive outing" for his friends in a padded school bus floating over Niagara Falls. His top priority, however, is to set the world free-fall record by parachuting from a helium balloon at 130,000 feet. It will require a pressurized suit to keep his blood from boiling and a temperature-control device to prevent his freezing in space or burning up on re-entry to the atmosphere. Weston and Keeling are still working on the designs.

Journey to the Stone Age

Thrusting from the island of New Guinea's steamy equatorial jungle, a snow-capped mountain pierces its perpetual shroud of mist. Deep in the mountain's shadow live a Stone Age people, the Dani. To them, the peak is Dugundugu, which is also their word for white and ice. They believe the mountain's ice offers strength, like the white meat of their pigs.

To THE INDONESIANS who rule Irian Jaya (the western portion of New Guinea, the world's second largest island after Greenland), the mountain is Puncak Jaya or "Victory Peak." And to the Western world, it's Carstensz Pyramid, after the Dutch explorer Jan Carstensz, who described it from his ship in 1623 during a rare break in the fog. Naming the peak was one thing. Getting there took more than three hundred years. In 1914, a British expedition of 262 people spent fifteen months inching just thirty miles into the jungle. Following the expedition, A. F. R. Wollaston reported to Britain's Alpine Club: "Even if we spent twice that time in the country, I doubt if we should have come as far as the foot of the highest range."

Indeed, the first foreigners to climb 16,023-foot Carstensz were Heinrich Harrer and team in 1962. They made first ascents of the three highest summits while getting to know the Dani people of the surrounding jungle. In his book *I come from the Stone Age*, Harrer evocatively describes the climbs and the year he spent among the people he described as "gentle cannibals." Gentle from his own interactions. Cannibals by reputation.

While cannibalism on the island of New Guinea is a fact, the local evidence is unclear. In the late 1960s a Harvard-Peabody anthropology expedition lived with the Dani near Wamena, two hundred miles from Carstensz Pyramid. They discovered piles of bones that seemed to imply occasional cannibalism; and the Dani, when pressed, would admit that perhaps such deeds happened. Mostly, though, the team described constant ritual warfare, with men of rival villages gathering on a hillside to fight with sharpened sticks. The fight ends as soon as someone is mortally wounded, with the losers fleeing to their home territory. Before long, however, both groups begin preparing for the next battle—deaths must be avenged to appease the spirits. Such battles have since been stopped by missionaries and government soldiers.

In 1962, the Dutch turned over control of Irian Jaya to Indonesia. For reasons still unclear, the new proprietors closed access to the entire Carstensz Pyramid area. Perhaps the Indonesians didn't want visitors to think their country primitive. Perhaps there was too much truth to rumors of fighting between natives and Indonesian troops.

In any case, the effect was to limit the Dani's contact with the outside world to a few missionaries. Until the late 1970s, those Dani inhabiting remote areas close to the mountain had almost no contact at all. In 1979, Britishers Peter Boardman and Hillary Collins arranged for a missionary pilot to land them illegally near the mountain. They returned with wild stories about the natives—and an alluring photo of an unclimbed two-thousand-foot rock wall leading directly to the summit of Carstensz Pyramid. When I saw their slide show, I had to go.

While the Dangerous Sports Club followed their vision of adventure, Bob Shapiro and I went all out pursuing our dream of going to Carstensz Pyramid. We secured another A. C. Irvine Grant, sponsorship from the Oxford Exploration Society, and an American Alpine Club Young Mountaineers' fellowship. Unfortunately we were still several thousand dollars short of funding our trip to Irian Jaya. I joked with a friend who worked for *Time* magazine's London bureau and had previously abused his expense account on my behalf, that he should cover our trip to New Guinea for the magazine. He sent off a letter to his editors in New York who promptly told him to get stuffed; but they did pass the proposal on to *Sports Illustrated*. Two weeks later we received a telex saying that *Sports Illustrated* would pay all of our expenses if they could send a reporter along with us.

Our timing was perfect. Sam Moses, a former football star and professional motorcycle racer, was *Sports Illustrated*'s macho writer covering motor sports and the outdoors. He'd written a couple of pieces on climbing and had been wanting to go on a mountaineering expedition when my friend's letter was passed to him. Before committing he checked a local climbing shop. In the front of the information section of *Mountain* magazine, the world's authority on climbing, the headline read, "Shapiro and Tabin make the Coveted First Free Ascent of Mount Kenya's Diamond Buttress." He assumed we were legitimate and decided to go. Sam was given two months' leave from the magazine to train full time with a private guide and climbing instructor. The magazine gave us our airfare and a carte blanche to purchase any equipment that was required. Bob and I decided that we needed all new clothing and gear. The plan was for Sam to train until the last possible moment. Bob and I would go to Indonesia and arrange permits and transportation and telex for Sam to come when everything was set. He would then fly to meet us with the equipment and expense money.

Bob and I finished our exams at Oxford, celebrated in England and Singapore, and reached Jakarta to find that it was impossible to obtain permits to go to the interior of Irian Jaya in 1980. We did succeed in getting fancy endorsements with letterhead and official stamps from the U.S. and British embassies and the head of the Indonesian Sports Federation. Encouraged, we wired Sam to join us, telling him, "Everything is perfect, permits no problem, come immediately!" expecting that our impressive papers would overwhelm the minor officials in Irian Jaya. Once we reached Jayapura we discovered that the Carstensz area was completely closed. Our imposing documents made us much too important for any official to risk his career sanctioning our going into an area where they believed we would certainly be killed and eaten. The chief of police, Mr. Bimbang, said he would give us a *Surat Jalan*, or walking papers, if the governor gave written permission. The governor said we needed a letter from the head of military intelligence, which is an oxymoron anywhere, but particularly in Indonesia. The director of military intelligence, in turn, referred us back to the chief of police.

On the day of Sam's arrival in Irian Jaya, Bob went to the airstrip to meet him while I made a last-ditch effort to find a way into the interior. The police chief begged me to go just to Wamena, a lowland Dani village in the Baliem valley, where there was a military outpost. He assured me that we could see the naked savages and that he would be able to guarantee our safety. I then met Leroy Kelm, a pilot who had flown in Vietnam and for Air America in Cambodia and Laos and now flew for the Missionary Air Fellowship. Leroy had flown Peter Boardman and greeted me warmly when I came to his office. He said that he didn't need a permit. He had a landing strip right at his house and he'd happily fly us to the village nearest to Carstensz Pyramid.

Success! I met Bob and Sam back at our sweltering thatched bamboo room in Jayapura. Sam had been traveling for thirty-six hours and was in no mood for jokes or bad news. Bob had judiciously failed to mention that we could not get permits. I blurted that Leroy would fly us illegally and Sam hit the roof. He accused us of lying to him and lying to *Sports Illustrated*. He said that he represented a very important magazine and the country of America and that he would not under any circumstances break the law.

In the midst of a tirade about how he would break every bone in our bodies and then bring us back to America to face the full fury of the law, he glanced down and saw my feet, clad in sandals. On my last night at Oxford my girlfriend had painted my toenails saying, "You might remember me a bit longer if I paint your toenails, mightn't you?" I thought it was romantic and let her go ahead. Sam stopped and stared at the lustrous red on my right foot and bright blue polish on the left. This trip was not shaping up as he expected. Suddenly it occurred to me that Sam didn't read Indonesian. I had a solution. Trying not to sound too patronizing, I affected an attitude of great astonishment that he should be so upset, explaining that he had completely misunderstood. What I'd actually meant to say was that we'd have the permits tomorrow.

The next day I went to Chief Bimbang, gave him a hefty bribe, and said we'd take the *Surat Jalan* to Wamena. I then rushed to Leroy Kelm, explained the situation to him, and he agreed to back me up. I then proudly showed the permits to Sam. The following morning Bob Shapiro, Sam Moses, and I bounced down a grass runway at Leroy Kelm's home outside of Jayapura, the capital of Irian Jaya. Our Aerocommander lifted off, bound for Ilaga, the closest Dani village to Carstensz Pyramid. We droned inland over an endless expanse of jungle-green hills furrowed with jagged, twisting canyons. The peaks grew larger and more dramatic as we neared the Carstensz Massif; flat land was nowhere to be seen.

We wing over a few clusters of round brown huts and terraced fields clinging to the steep green walls. "There's no landing strip," Leroy drawls. "I'll try to put her down in that sweet potato patch." He points to an ominously tiny clearing on a hillside above a group of huts. He noses the plane into a sickening dive, muttering the Lord's Prayer under his breath. My terror mounts as we swoop toward the sloping, muddy field.

We touch down softly enough, but Leroy's wide-eyed look says something is seriously wrong. The plane doesn't slow down; instead it skids on the mud as if it were ice. The end of the clearing looms closer at an alarming rate. We slide diagonally until one tire sticks in the mud, and spin violently to a halt with the left wingtip fifteen feet from the drop-off to an oblivion of jungle.

As Leroy chops the engine and silence washes over us, my heart races with giddy relief. But when I look around, new sights and sounds electrify me with a jolt of adrenaline. From all sides, men and boys come at us, screaming a guttural "oooh-whah, oooh-whah," with their voices cracking to a falsetto on the "whah." Each carries a spear or a stone. All are naked except for a *kebowak*, or penis gourd, which they pound with their palms, drumming a resonant counterpoint to their shrieks. They surround the plane, pounding and screeching.

Leroy steps out, a big grin splitting his silver muttonchop sideburns. He makes eye contact with a couple of Dani in the front. They return bright, toothy smiles. Sam tapes their chanting on a small cassette recorder, and when he plays it back the sounds break the ice completely. Dani boys close in around us, yelling and singing, curiosity filling their eyes.

Below us stretch terraced sweet potato fields, some only fifteen feet wide, linked by footpaths down to a central group of dwellings. Scattered on the surrounding slopes are a smattering of round huts and other fields carved out of the foliage. Further below and all around, tangled rain forest hems the inhabited land. Here in the high foothills, warm tropical air sweeps up to meet cool mountain breezes, creating a zone of near-constant mist and precipitation.

Leroy's inventive pantomime organizes a group of Dani men to wrestle his plane out of the mud. We unload our packs and he hops aboard, revs the engines, and takes off, leaving the three of us to find our way to the mountain. We have a two-hundred-word Dani vocabulary list from the Harvard anthropologists and ten loads of gear. We hope to enlist ten Dani men as porters to haul it all to the base of Carstensz Pyramid—or Dugundugu, as we understand in the Dani tongue. For payment we've brought ten steel axe-heads, ten bags of salt, ten bags of sugar, and ten Boy Scout knives.

We embark on our own wild game of charades trying to explain what we want. Only three of our Dani words seem familiar to these Ilaga villagers, two hundred miles from the tribesmen whom the anthropologists studied. We draw pictures and show photographs of the mountain. One older man, Seppanous, becomes very excited and demands my pen. I hand it to him. He immediately removes the *am whyak*, or boar's tusk, from his nose and proudly inserts the pen.

We sit on the ground amid a cluster of thatched huts, negotiating, gesticulating, laughing. The women go bare-breasted, wearing only beads and loose grass skirts. Naked infants and the children play in the mud around us. Pigs, their only domesticated animals, roam freely. Women carrying stone hoes walk past on their way to and from the fields. A few steel axes are the only visible sign that we aren't entirely in the Stone Age.

We are at eight thousand feet, and despite our proximity to the equator, when it clouds over and rains, I feel chilled. The naked Dani seem perfectly comfortable and a bit amused as I search for my rain top.

Eventually we think we've struck an agreement: ten men will carry our loads and escort us through the jungle to Dugundugu. After a night of singing we hand out ten equally weighted packs. To our horror, the Dani rip the bags open and spread gear all over the ground. Villagers come by, picking from our things. Bob, Sam, and I stare at each other in disbelief, amazed at how quickly our climb is over. As we watch helplessly, dozens of men, women, and children gather up our belongings and file out into the forest, chanting a song.

We're left with no choice. We get up and follow the merry expedition past the farthest cultivated fields and into the cool, dark jungle. We wander under a canopy of dense foliage, sometimes in thick mud, sometimes on rotting logs suspended high above the ground, always on trails that I could never follow on my own. At first, the compass says we are traveling north; a few minutes later it reads south. Before long, we put the maps away and just walk along, hoping we are hiking toward Dugundugu.

After five hours we stop in a small clearing. The Dani spread out, shouting and laughing, each taking on a task. Some gather firewood while others chop at large trees with stone axes. Yoni, a graceful athletic young man, takes dry moss out of his *kebowak* and strikes two flints together, catching the spark in the moss. He blows gently, puts the glowing pile on the ground, covers it with wet wood, and fans it into roaring flame.

Women take Pandanus fronds, break the tips, and pull single strands from the fibrous palm leaf to make instant organic needles with thread. Then they sew the fronds together to make a waterproof covering for their shelter. When a giant oak is about to topple, great debate ensues about where it will fall. As it comes down, much "oooh-whah-ing" and pounding on the *kebowaks* accompanies the descent. By the time we set up our tent, the Dani have built a wooden hut covered with a waterproof layer of Pandanus leaves.

Minutes later, Martinus, one of the older men, sees me struggling to boil water on my pack stove. He returns with a pot of boiling water. I thank him with a piece of chocolate and watch, amazed, as he takes only a tiny nibble and then brings it around so everyone can have a taste. At night they build a huge fire in their shelter with the flames licking at the wooden roof. Songs and laughter radiate from the smoky hut well into the night.

As I observe the Dani, they observe me. They are fascinated by miracles (like zippers) that I take for granted. But I see no sign of jealousy, either toward us or among themselves. Not a single item of ours will disappear. When the stronger Dani men drop their loads at the top of hills, they go back to help the older and slower members.

Their emotions seem very close to the surface. Displeasure shows quickly, often evoking tears. But moments later, the same two people embrace and laugh. They are constantly amused by my struggles to adapt to the changing environment and care for myself with all my bulky possessions.

Every day I grow more amazed by our companions. We mountaineers are immediately dependent on them for our directions. By the second night they bring us water, fire, and other necessities—treating us like children who have not yet learned to care for themselves. When I try to kindle the sopping wet wood using a lighter and finally fuel from my stove—all without success—Yoni watches knowingly from a distance. Just as my frustration peaks, he walks over, plucks a clump of moss from his *kebowak*, strikes two pieces of flint, blows, piles on soaked wood, blows some more, and stands back, smiling at the blaze.

I come to see that the Dani live in utter harmony with the rugged, hilly rain forest. The forest meets their needs as surely as the malls provide ours at home. Most of their diet consists of fire-roasted *mbee*, or sweet potatoes, which they carry in *yums*, orchid-decorated woven reed bags that hang from their foreheads down their backs. But they also gather roots, grubs, and insects to eat as we walk.

On our third day in the jungle, Wanimbo, a tall athletic Dani in his mid-twenties, presents me with a live bat he's holding by the feet. He smiles gently; I flinch away. With a shrug he takes an arrow, pushes it into the bat's anus and sticks it into the fire. A few minutes later he carefully divides the meat among everyone.

Twenty-four Dani stay with us for the full ten days it takes to reach Dugundugu. In the last days, we climb steep, muddy hills to finally emerge from the forest onto the expansive Ngorilong Plateau, a flat, moss-covered bog. At twelve thousand feet, our naked escorts stay warm with frequent fires and Pandanus-leaf ponchos made on the spot. We cross a snow-covered, sharp-cobbled limestone pass at nearly fifteen thousand feet; they all pad along barefoot.

No one seems surprised to see snow; they have clearly come this way before. I wonder why naked people would climb to a snowy mountain. Perhaps the easiest trade route involves climbing through the high mountain passes rather than fighting thick jungle. Unfortunately, we are still communicating through gestures and I cannot ask such a complex question.

In the end, we succeed in making our planned first ascent on Carstensz and a few other fine climbs besides. And while I came for these routes, the real experience was the privilege of spending time with the Dani. To their mountains we have brought the latest in Gore-Tex rainwear, freeze-dried foods, high tech everything. Still, we are humbled by our Stone Age companions. With one stitch of a palm-leaf needle, one strike of a flint against *kebowak*-dry moss, I learn how much we have sacrificed in our modern world.

Kangshung 1981—Everest's Unclimbed East Face

MOUNT EVEREST IS A THREE-SIDED PYRAMID lying on the border between Nepal and Tibet, rising to a height of 29,028 feet above sea level. The first reconnaissance of Mount Everest with a view to climbing the peak was the British expedition of 1921 with George Leigh Mallory as one of the principal explorer-climbers. Mallory made an excellent topographical map of the mountain and was the first Westerner to walk up the Kangshung glacier and gaze upon Mount Everest's largest and steepest face. His report was not encouraging. He wrote:

We had already by this hour taken the time to observe the great Eastern Face of Mount Everest, and more particularly the lower edge of the hanging glacier: it required but little further gazing to be convinced, to know, that almost everywhere the rocks below must be exposed to ice falling from the glacier; that if, elsewhere, it might prove possible to climb up, the performance would be too arduous, would take too much time, and lead to no convenient platform; that, in short, other men, less wise, might attempt this way if they would, but, emphatically, it was not for us.

Mallory then moved around to the north where he discovered what he felt to be a feasible route. He returned in 1923 to attempt the northern approach to Mount Everest. After a failed first attempt he made plans to return the next year. When a reporter asked him why he was attempting to climb Mount Everest, Mallory replied, "Because it's there!" In 1924, with Andrew C. Irvine (for whom the A. C. Irvine Grant is endowed), Mallory disappeared high on the slopes of Mount Everest. The mountain remained virginal until May 29, 1953, when Sir

Edmund Hillary and Tenzing Norgay Sherpa reached the summit via the mountain's south side from Nepal. In 1960, Wang Fu Chow and his Chinese compatriots, climbing in a large national expedition, made the first ascent of Mallory's route on the north side of Everest. In 1963 the first Americans reached the summit of Mount Everest with Tom Hornbein and Willy Unsoeld climbing the technically challenging West Ridge, which delineates the border between Nepal and Tibet. In 1975 Chris Bonington's British expedition achieved a breakthrough in climbing difficulty on Everest when they scaled the imposing and sustained Southwest Face. Three years later Peter Habeler and Reinhold Messner succeeded in making the first climb of Mount Everest without supplemental oxygen, and a Polish expedition climbed the mountain in winter. By 1979 every face and ridge on two thirds of the mountain had been climbed. The mountain had also been climbed solo and during the monsoon. But the largest and steepest side of Mount Everest, the massive Kangshung, or East Face, had still not been approached.

Meanwhile, the Chinese government was changing its policy toward outsiders. China had annexed Tibet in 1950. The Dalai Lama, the theocratic ruler of the country, fled into exile in India. China kept Tibet a completely restricted area. In 1979 the Chinese gave a permit for a Japanese expedition to enter Tibet to attempt Mount Everest from the north. Rumor was that they were soon to open Tibet to Western climbers. Dick Blum, the husband of Senator Dianne Feinstein (then-mayor of San Francisco), was a keen trekker who had walked in the Nepal Himalayas on several occasions. He was about to depart for a friendship trip to China with his wife when American climber Eric Perlman suggested that he request a permit for Americans to attempt the Chinese approaches to Mount Everest. The timing was perfect. Blum was in the right place at the right time. The Chinese government granted the first permit for an American expedition to climb in Tibet.

Blum asked Lou Reichardt, a well-known Himalayan climber from San Francisco, to help plan the climb. The permit would allow an assault on the mountain from any side. Reichardt had seen a photograph taken from the top of neighboring Makalu, the world's fifth highest peak. From the photo he thought there might be a feasible route up Everest's East Face. Perlman argued that the object was to climb the mountain and that the best chance of success lay in the north. Meanwhile Blum had enlisted the help of Sir Edmund Hillary whom he knew from his charitable work with Hillary's Himalayan Foundation. Hillary stated that, "if the Americans climb Mount Everest from the north it will just be another ascent of the mountain, but a climb from the east will be history." With this in mind Andrew Harvard, an experienced expedition mountaineer who was already in China, was dispatched to do a reconnaissance of the East Face of Everest. Traveling with a Chinese interpreter and liaison officer, he journeyed to Tibet and trekked to Mount Everest. Andy became the second outsider to view the face. Based on improvements in equipment and techniques he felt it would be difficult, "probably the hardest climb ever attempted," but possible, to scale the East Face of Mount Everest.

With the objective established, the next tasks were fund-raising and team selection. Blum, a professional financier by trade, remained expedition leader while Reichardt was named climbing leader on the mountain. Sir Edmund Hillary joined the effort as a special expedition advisor who would accompany the team to base camp. The team that was selected was a who's who of the best American climbers in 1980. In addition to Eric Perlman, Andy Harvard, and Lou Reichardt, the group included the current hot Himalayan superstar, John Roskelley; the tandem responsible for the hardest alpine ascents in North America, George Lowe and Chris Jones; a top Alaskan guide in Gary Bocarde; and arguably the two top rockjocks, Jim Bridwell and Henry Barber. Also on the initial team were Sue Giller, an excellent Himalayan climber; two experienced climbing doctors, Jim Morrissey and Dan Reid; and Bruce McCubbry, a solid Bay area mountaineer. The fund-raising went smoothly. Many people and organizations, including ABC television sports, were eager to be involved in the historic ascent.

A few months before departure Jim Bridwell decided that he could not go on the expedition. The team began looking for a replacement. Because most of the expedition members were in their thirties or forties it was suggested that they might choose a strong rock climber under twenty-five. This happened at the same time that Sam Moses' two-part article appeared in *Sports Illustrated*. When I first heard Sam's account of our trip to Irian Jaya was going to be published I had some trepidation. I had no idea how he perceived me. We had become friends during the trip and I had led our team up the climb. However, Sam never seemed comfortable with my painted toenails. I also had donned a *kebowak* for part of our approach march, ate insects when the Dani did, carried three penis gourds to the top of Carstensz Pyramid, and insisted Sam and Bob strip naked for a *kebowak* summit photo despite a raging blizzard. In addition, Sam found out that he had been deceived about the *Surat Jalan* when we were arrested upon our return from the mountain.

Although he did describe me as "cheerfully oblivious to society's norms," Sam's articles made me out to be incredibly energetic and enthusiastic: "Geoff was up there on the leading end of the rope, the 'sharp end,' as climbers call it, often unprotected, 800 feet off the ground, standing on tiny edges and clinging to a wall of rock while icy water dribbled down his sleeves to his armpits." Moreover, he mentioned that a Kowloon fortune teller had said that I was the "luckiest sonofabitch" he had ever seen, which is a good attribute to have on an expedition. Sam's article got me noticed, and no one on the team knew me well enough to say anything negative. Finally, Bruce McCubbry was a friend of my father's and actively supported my candidacy.

I had enrolled in Harvard Medical School in the fall of 1980. My focus was on becoming a doctor, and I had no plans for big climbing adventures in the near future. This idea was further enforced six weeks later when I was bouldering without a rope at a small outcrop just outside of Boston called Hammond Pond. A rock broke off while I was climbing an overhanging route. I was only fifteen feet off the ground, but I had my foot hooked up above my head so that when my handhold pulled loose I torpe-doed straight down, breaking my left arm and knocking myself unconscious. Fortunately, I was with a medical school classmate named Hansel Stedman who saved my life when I stopped breathing. Hansel gave me mouth to nose resuscitation and kept me breathing while carrying me a few hundred yards to the road, where he flagged down a motorist who took me to New-ton-Wellesley Hospital. I remained in a coma for thirty-six hours and spent a week in the hospital. I struggled to catch up with my medical studies while having continued problems with short-term memory and concentration. By second semester I was back to doing some rock climbing on the weekends. With the help of the medical school I had nearly caught up with my classes.

In the spring of 1981 I was studying for a pharmacology exam when Lou Reichardt called to ask if I would be interested in joining the team that was going to attempt the last unclimbed face on Mount Everest. Lou would be in Boston the following week and wanted to know if I could meet him for lunch. I was bouncing off the walls with excitement. I would have been over-joyed just to have lunch with Lou Reichardt. The people on the team were the heroes whom I had been reading about. Reichardt was America's best high-altitude mountaineer. I knew of the tragedy on Dhaulagiri when he had been the only person to survive an avalanche that killed six of his teammates, and of his successful ascent of the mountain two years later. I had read of his exploits on Nanda Devi and how he made the first ascent of K2 without supplemental oxygen. And now he wanted to talk to me about joining him to climb Mount Everest. It would probably ruin my medical career. I knew that I was not experi-enced enough for that kind of climb: the biggest mountain I had been on was 17,000-foot Mount Kenya. I was also in the worst shape of my life. I instantly replied, "YES!"

I put on my faded pile jacket, my Peruvian herder's cap, and painter's pants, trying to look like the kind of experienced climber he would want for his expedition, and went to meet Lou

Reichardt on the steps of Harvard Medical School. I arrived early and waited. The only other person on the steps was a long, gangly man with checked polyester pants, a striped polyester shirt that was a size too small, and thick glasses that were fogged, filthy, and sitting askew on his nose. With large, open-mouthed bites he was eating a tuna fish submarine sandwich. I was looking desperately for the great mountaineer when, with a big tuna fish smile, Lou Reichardt warmly extended his hand and said, "Geoff?"

Lou went back to California telling me that I would be considered for the team. A few weeks later I was told that they had chosen Kim Momb, a top young climber from Spokane, Washington. I was selected as an alternate. The week before the team departed I called Lou and Jim Morrissey, wished them good luck, and thanked them for considering me. Then, several days after the team was supposed to have left, I received a phone call from a man who introduced himself as Scott MacBeth, the team's base camp manager. Scott explained that he was delayed in his departure because of a blood infection and hadn't left with the rest of the group. He said one of the other climbers, Henry Barber, had not gone at the last minute because of personal reasons. "Do you still want to go to Everest?" he asked.

"What?! YES!!!" I answered. I was soaring ten feet off the ground. I made a quick phone call to the dean of students and told him that I had just been invited to go to attempt the last unclimbed face of Mount Everest. I'd be leaving medical school, and would be returning in December. Inexplicably, the dean was not as excited as my climbing friends. He said that it was impossible for me to go. I tried to explain that this was Everest. He replied, "Yes, and other students like to go to the beach on their vacations. What's the difference?"

Now a full two and a half weeks behind the rest of the team, Scott and I flew from San Francisco to Beijing. Scott turned out to be an ideal traveling companion, and our Chinese hosts most hospitable. Unfortunately, the transportation into Tibet was not regular at that time. Moreover, Scott was as interested in seeing the sights of China as in getting to the mountain. The days in

Beijing rolled on. We were guests at wonderful banquet after wonderful banquet. The meals lasted for hours with dozens of courses and toasts of Mao Tai liquor between each dish. We took trips out to the Ming tombs and the Great Wall of China, and explored the Forbidden City and other tourist sites of Beijing. We wandered the streets early in the morning watching the city awaken with Tai Chi, felt the bustle of the days, and rode bicycles through the town in the late afternoon, absorbing the sounds and smells before our evening banquet. It was fun, but my mind was on Everest. I was concerned about my role on the team, nervous about meeting my teammates, anxious about climbing in the Himalayas, worried about my own acclimatization, and a bit more impatient than Scott. Finally, after six days, we boarded a plane to Chengdu in the Szechuan Province. We encountered similar delays in Chengdu before finally being shuttled out to an old Russian turboprop. The flight took us over a seemingly endless array of immense, shimmering rock and ice peaks. I kept my face pressed to the window throughout the spectacular four-hour trip, over hundreds of miles of uncharted Himalayan mountains, to land in Lhasa, Tibet.

Lhasa was a place of contrasts in 1981. Physically, it was beautiful. Softly colored, hills rose on all sides of the city and golden statues glistened from the rooftops of the temples and monasteries. On a hill above town, the traditional home of the Dalai Lama, the Potala Palace, dominated the architecture of the city and projected a feeling of grandeur to everything below. Traditionally clad Tibetans chanted mantras and spun prayer wheels as they went about their business. Yet, the tension between the Tibetans and their Chinese conquerors was palpable. All of the main religious buildings were completely shut down with only Chinese guards outside. The smiles vanished from Tibetan faces as they passed Chinese soldiers. There were no tourist hotels in Lhasa at the time, so we were housed in an army barracks on the edge of town. We spent several days wandering through the city. It felt awkward to be allowed access to the monasteries and temples that the faithful were denied. We visited the deserted Jokang temple which had previously been the main shrine for the people of Tibet. In the Potala Palace the artwork and ornate golden statues were beautiful beyond my imagination, yet there was an eerie feeling walking alone through the vast 999 rooms with only the occasional glowering Han Chinese soldier sharing the sacred building.

We were delayed another week in Lhasa waiting for transportation. By this time I was fully enjoying Scott's company, his knowledge of the region, and his explanations of Tibetan Buddhism. I learned that Siddhartha believed that there are four essential truths: "Man suffers; suffering comes from unfulfilled desires; one can eliminate suffering by overcoming desire; and to overcome desire one must follow the eightfold path to wisdom." I finally began to adopt a Buddhist attitude of acceptance. Things were the way they were and I couldn't rush the trip. I became absorbed in David Snellgrove and Hugh Richardson's wonderful text, *A Cultural History of Tibet*, in reading about Mahayana Buddhism, and in trying to understand the changes in Tibet since the Chinese invaded.

After a week in Lhasa, Scott and I were given a jeep and a driver and set out along the arid Tibetan plateau. Our first stop was Xigatse, the second city of Tibet, with its impressive Drepung monastery. From there we drove on a heavily rutted dirt road to Xegar, the site of the Xegar Dzong, a hillside fortress that was the last outpost of Tibetan resistance to the Chinese invasion in 1953. The Tibetan landscape unfolded before us with a long, arid, richly textured plateau stretching to the horizon in one direction and the spine of the Himalayan range on the other side of our jeep. Unfortunately, the mountains were socked in with monsoon clouds, and we had no views of the highest peaks. The monsoons sweep north from India and hit the high Himalayan peaks where they drop their precipitation, leaving the Tibetan plateau a harsh thirteen-thousand-foot desert.

From Xegar, Scott and I followed a winding single track that wove into the mountains with precipitous drops at every curve until we finally arrived at the small yak-herding village of Kharta. We were given three yaks and a yak driver to help us with our seven-day trek to Mount Everest, which proved to be one of the greatest hikes of my life. Glimmering twenty-thousand-foot peaks rose up on all sides. I was mesmerized. I was overwhelmed by the scale. The jagged summits floated a vertical mile and a half above us. At every turn in the trail the views changed, becoming even more dramatic. We walked over a high pass adorned with prayer flags and dropped into the lush Kama Valley. We descended to a small wooded camp with beautiful rhododendrons in full bloom from the monsoon storms. The trail then wove back upward into the world of rock, snow, and ice to join the Kangshung Glacier at sixteen thousand feet. Nothing I had ever seen prepared me for the grandeur of the highest Himalayan peaks. The icy walls of Chomolonzo glistened in the morning sun and Makalu rose twelve thousand feet vertically above us as we came out onto the glacier. We followed the side of the glacier for one day on our way toward base camp before we were able to see the East Face of Mount Everest and the North Face of Lhotse in the distance. Both rise over two vertical miles. The sheer mass and beauty would have taken my breath away, had I not already been gasping from the altitude.

Looking up the glacier we were surprised to see people coming down. It turned out to be Dick Blum and an entourage of porters. Dick had decided he didn't enjoy life in base camp and was leaving the expedition. I thought it was strange that the expedition leader was leaving. I was also a bit worried as Dick seemed to have no knowledge that Scott had invited me along.

We walked only a few more hours before we ran into the next group of people descending the trail. I instantly recognized Sir Edmund Hillary from his photographs. He was staggering along the path with a bloody bandage wrapped around his head. The man with Hillary warmly greated Scott and, after being introduced, I too was enthusiastically welcomed by Dr. Jim Morrissey. Sir Edmund Hillary then turned to me and asked, "Are you driving the bus?"

Morrissey explained that Hillary had developed a slight case of cerebral edema, had fallen and struck his head, and then rolled over, contaminating the open wound in fresh yak dung. The gash in his scalp had become infected. Morrissey was terrified that our expedition would only be remembered for killing Sir Edmund Hillary. He was rushing Hillary down to lower altitude, expecting to take him to Beijing where he would receive additional medical care. Despite a dirty rag wrapped around his head and an altered mental state, Hillary had the carriage of a great man. I had read many books by and about him. Beyond making the first ascent of Everest and his impressive climbing resume, Hillary had traversed Antarctica, been to both the North and South Poles, built schools and hospitals for the Sherpa people, started his own foundation to help the indigenous populations of the Himalayas, and served as New Zealand High Commissioner to India and Nepal. He was one of my heroes. Yet, despite his illness, I was even more impressed than I expected to be by Hillary, the man. He had a quiet warmth that emanated from his dazed eyes. I asked him to pose for a picture. He smiled gamely and wished me luck on the climb before stumbling on down the trail.

Two days later we walked into base camp. It was obviously not a happy place. I tented my first night with John Roskelley. Roskelley had distinguished himself with the hardest climbs of any American over the past several years and had recently been hailed by the media and the top European climber, Reinhold Messner, as the greatest mountaineer in the world. I knew of his bold climbs in the Himalayas, including the first ascents of several technically difficult peaks as well as the first American climb of K2, and I was eager to learn from him. As I crawled into our tent, slightly in awe, John Roskelley's only words to me were, "This face is suicide. If you climb on this route, Geoff, you are going to die," before he rolled over and went to sleep.

I lay awake all night. This was not turning out like I had expected. The expedition leader had left, Sir Edmund Hillary had high-altitude sickness, and our route was too dangerous for John Roskelley. Before morning I was aware of what a great adventure I had already had and how privileged I was to be in Tibet and seeing these mountains. I attempted to push my preconceptions out of my conscious thoughts, keep an open mind, and flow with the adventure.

The East Face of Everest is enormous. There was no consensus over what was a feasible or safe route. One faction, spearheaded by Chris Jones, wanted to follow the ridge that makes up the north side of the buttress. Jones felt that this would be much easier climbing and afford a feasible route to the upper snow slopes. A second group felt that Jones' line was suicidal because of avalanche danger. This team, led by George Lowe, was trying to push a very difficult direct route up the sheer initial five-thousand-vertical-foot rock and ice buttress. Roskelley felt that Lowe's route was impossibly hard. The vertical mile of technical difficulties was insurmountable. And, even if it proved possible to climb the buttress, he was certain the slopes above were suicidal, with unreasonable avalanche danger. Roskelley argued that Jones' proposed route was ridiculous, being suicidal the entire way. He strongly advocated going around to the easier and safer north side to make a successful climb on Mount Everest. Andy Harvard told me to ignore Roskelley. He said that John, as a professional climber, needed to reach the top of the mountain for his reputation, and wanted to do what was easiest and best for himself. While the arguments raged, Lou Reichardt, our climbing leader, avoided the controversy and led by simply carrying heavy loads, often making double carries in a single day, to support whatever activity was going on up on the mountain.

I was shocked to see my heroes bickering and confused about what to do. Adding to my discomfort was a feeling that I was in over my head, even if the route were climbable. Base camp sat at an altitude of seventeen thousand feet, the same as my previous high point. I felt the pulse pounding in my temples and became short of breath with moderate exertion. I was worried that my physical skills were not in the same league as any of the superstars on the team. I rested a week before moving seven miles across the Kangshung Glacier to our advanced base camp. I decided that I should at least check things out for myself before making any decision. On the day that I moved to advanced base camp, Roskelley made an impassioned plea on the radio for Kim Momb to come down. He said, "I brought you on this trip, Kim. I owe it to your family. Don't let me down. You must come home alive. Come off the mountain at once if you want to live. I'm getting out of here tomorrow. Walk out with me. Please!" I met Kim Momb for the first time as he was retreating off of the mountain. We briefly shook hands before he, Bruce McCubbry, and Roskelley, left.

Meanwhile, the climbing team pushed along Lowe's route toward the top of the initial vertical buttress. The climbing was hard, at a level of technical difficulty never before attempted on a peak the scale of Mount Everest. There were pitches of vertical ice, arduous free climbing, and very strenuous overhanging aid climbing on crumbly schist where the only progress that could be made was by pounding pitons into the friable rock and pulling oneself up on these insecure anchors. George Lowe was doing the majority of the leading on the hardest sections. Also working on the route were Eric Perlman, Gary Bocarde, Sue Giller, Dan Reid, and ABC cameraman David Breashears. An enormous avalanche had swept over the ridge that Jones had suggested. Fortunately no one was in its path. All climbing efforts were now concentrated on the "Lowe Buttress" route.

I rested a few days at advanced base camp listening eagerly to stories of what had happened on the mountain. I was particularly fascinated by the tales of Dan Reid. He was supposed to be a team physician, but when they needed help on the route he headed right up. I heard about how he had attempted to solo climb a vertical icicle, and had taken several long falls, self-belayed on a single knife blade piton, before finally giving up on a stormy day when no one else was willing to climb. This pitch later became known as Reid's Nemesis.

When I started up the fixed ropes, I was amazed by the difficulty of the climbing that the team had accomplished. The leaders installed permanent ropes which I followed using mechanical ascenders that slide up the rope but catch and lock when weighted downward. I spent a night at Snow Camp, the first camp on the mountain, which was located below a snow ridge leading up to the ice gully where much of the debris from the upper face funneled down. Unfortunately, the gully was the only line of weakness in a series of impassable mushroomed snow ridges, and our only possible route to the upper headwall. The worst time to be on this part of the buttress was in the afternoon, when the sun warmed the upper face. The heat melted the ice into water which seeped into cracks. At night, the water froze and expanded. The next day the warming loosened adhesions, and rock eroded down the mountain into the gully. They called the chute the "Bowling Alley," as bowling-ball-sized pieces of rock and ice ricocheted through every day as soon as the upper face was touched by the sun. I left very early in the morning and then raced as quickly as possible, like a scared rabbit, up the seven-hundred-foot, sixty-degree ice chasm to reach the camp on top of the chute, aptly named Pinsetter Camp.

At Pinsetter Camp I met Dan Reid for the first time. This slightly built man projected an incredible energy. He had a wide grin, scraggly beard, and through his granny glasses his eyes focussed intensely on anyone he was speaking to. He spoke matter-of-factly, saying that he thought the Bowling Alley was over-rated and that I shouldn't be scared because "when it's your time to go, it's your time to go and there's nothing you can do about it."

Meanwhile Eric Perlman and Gary Bocarde had just reached the Helmet Camp, on top of the buttress at 21,500 feet. Gary, a veteran mountain guide on Mount McKinley, observed the crevasses stretching out above and declared the upper face to be unclimbable. He and Eric then retreated off the mountain, saying they were not going to climb any more. Similarly, Sue Giller decided the risks were too great to venture higher. Chris Jones had broken some ribs with a high-altitude coughing fit and was unable to climb, Andy Harvard was sick, and the film crew had pulled back. Thus, there were only four of us still on the mountain willing to move upward. These were Lou Reichardt, George Lowe, Dan Reid, and me. We discussed our options. George, who had done most of the difficult leading to that point and had been breaking through psychological barriers in the climbing world for fifteen years, felt that we should at least give it a try. Lou argued that it was not worth the risk. He pointed out that of the four of us, he was the only one who had been above twenty-three thousand feet previously without oxygen, and that I was still poorly acclimatized. Moreover, we had no support and only twelve days of supplies. Dan Reid then said that the only thing to do was to sign a death pact. If we all agreed that we should make a headlong dash for the summit, then one of us would most likely reach the top and get down alive, and we'd succeed on the first ascent on the East Face of Mount Everest. The death pact would state that if any one of us became sick or injured we wanted our partners to leave us to die so that they could make the top. As long as we signed a death pact he felt it would be legal. The other three of us looked at each other and realized that this expedition was over.

The next morning we began rappelling down the ropes. "Death-pact" Dan said he wanted to take one last look, and remained high on the mountain. George, Lou, and I descended through the Bowling Alley in the dark and waited at Snow Camp for Dan. We began to worry when the sun crept up onto the upper face, and were relieved when we heard Dan yodel as he approached the camp. Then, we saw that his right leg was completely red. His boot and lower leg were soaked through with blood. With a cheerful grin he said, "A couple of big ones came through while I was rappelling. I dodged most of 'em but one sucker got me." We pulled up his windpants leg and found that he had an implosion injury, exposing five inches of his tibia. We helped him down to advanced base camp, where we learned that Jim Morrissey had returned from successfully evacuating Sir Edmund Hillary back to Beijing. Jim looked at Dan's leg and decided it would not be possible to move him back to base camp. He would remain with Dan in advanced base camp after sewing Dan's leg closed in three layers with thirty-eight stitches.

The rest of the team began carrying loads back across the glacier from advanced base camp to base camp while we sent a messenger out for yaks to evacuate camp. While waiting for the yaks, George Lowe asked me if I would like to make a first ascent on a peak called Kartse, which dominates the vista behind base camp. George and I had a perfect day, climbing a beautiful, steep ridge in perfect sunshine and calm air to the 21,390-foot summit of Kartse. I was still floating on the summits as we walked back to base camp. I felt great on top of Kartse, had learned that George was not only a great climber but a great guy to climb with, and realized that with acclimatization I could climb with him.

We returned to find base camp in an uproar. Jim Morrissey had called on the radio to say that Dan Reid, after his week of resting at advanced base camp, had popped a handful of his own medications, thus earning a new nickname, "PercoDan," and solo climbed up the fixed ropes. Jim tried to catch him but did not have the technical climbing skill, and because of having to go down with Sir Edmund Hillary, he lacked Dan's acclimatization. Dan brought an unusual assortment of gear for his solo bid, including a stove but no fuel, so he was unable to melt water, and a considerable amount of food that all needed cooking. He also brought with him a tent but no sleeping bag. I had images in my mind of Dan limping into the clouds to disappear like George Leigh Mallory. He eventually returned, having climbed for thirty-six straight hours, saying that he had gone up to retrieve the Explorers' Club flag which he had left up at the high point, and to check out snow conditions for future years. It was the consensus of everyone that Dan Reid, one of the most wonderful and warmest people we had ever met, was completely nuts.

On the trek out our liaison officer, Wang Fu Chow, who had been the first Chinese man to summit Mount Everest, expressed sympathy that we had not made the summit. Wang Fu Chow had also made the first ascent of Mount Xixibangma, the only one of the world's fourteen highest mountains that is completely in Tibet. He matter-of-factly said that it would be possible for us to attempt to climb Mount Xixibangma. George Lowe, Eric Perlman, Lou Reichardt, Jim Morrissey, and I instantly took him up on the offer. We said good-bye to the rest of the team at Kharta and headed for Xixibangma.

Xixibangma is a peak that rises abruptly from the Tibetan plateau at fourteen thousand feet to just over twenty-six thousand feet with no intervening foothills. It is probably the most dramatic relief in the world. The route we tried is technically quite easy, following a low-angle ridge line to a steep ice slope that allows one to gain the final ridge. Unfortunately, the winter jetstream winds lowered to twenty-two thousand feet. George, Eric, and Lou were poised to go for the top when our high camp tent was ravaged by one-hundred-mile-an-hour gusts. It was impossible for our team to reach the summit. However, the team experience was absolutely perfect. We were perfectly together, shared a common attitude toward the climb, and had a lot of fun. On our way back to Lhasa we all decided that with the right team and knowing the route up the initial buttress, the East Face of Mount Everest could be climbed. Jim Morrissey decided to apply for a permit to return in two years to make the first ascent of the Kangshung Face. We reached Beijing and went to the Chinese mountaineering office where Jim gave a strong presentation saying that we had figured out the feasible route, and had done all the hard work, and that the Chinese should keep the route virginal until we were able to return to try it. The man smiled broadly and through an interpreter said, "No problem, Dr. Reid already have permit."

Everest 1983—The First Ascent of the Kangshung Face

I RETURNED FROM TIBET to find that I was out of medical school. I reapplied for admission and was reaccepted with the understanding that I would not leave again. Meanwhile, Dan Reid turned over the permit for the return to the Kangshung Face to Jim Morrissey, who assumed expedition leadership under the condition that Dan remain part of the next team. Dan agreed to just be a base camp doctor and assured Jim that he would not do anything dangerous. Jim was the perfect leader for this type of trip. He had a vast amount of expedition experience, lots of common sense, strong leadership skills, and, primarily a doctor rather than a climber, he did not have a climbing ego that would clash with his team. He was thus able to listen and weigh all options and then make a decision. Tall and powerful, Jim had a commanding personality and a strong sense of self-confidence that persuaded people to follow. Jim selected a team that he felt gave the best chance for success, blending top climbers who would work well together. The common attribute was a shared belief that the Kangshung Face could be climbed.

From the 1981 team he asked Dan Reid, Andy Harvard, Lou Reichardt, Kim Momb, George Lowe, and me to return to Everest with him in 1983. Adding to this nucleus of seven, Jim invited Carlos Buhler, Carl Tobin, David Coombs, Jay Cassell, David Cheesmond, and Chris Kopczynski. The result was not necessarily the best thirteen climbers in America in 1983, but very likely the best team America could have produced. A final addition was John Boyle, a banker, engineer, and yachtsman as base camp manager. The trip again was well funded, with *National Geographic* magazine as a principal sponsor.

Climbing the last unclimbed face on Everest had become a consuming romantic quest for me. I desperately wanted to go on the trip. However, there was no chance of Harvard Medical School giving me leave to go climbing again. Then, Michael Wiedman, a professor of eye surgery, approached me and proposed that we do a research project on the physiology of high altitude. In particular, Dr. Wiedman was interested in retinal hemorrhaging at high altitude and whether an ocular exam could be used as a prognosticator of high altitude cerebral or pulmonary edema. I was thus able to schedule a research elective and did not have to apply for a leave of absence. Beyond learning to perform ophthalmoscopy, I trained for the trip by running the five miles to and from my apartment to school every day, sprinting the steps of the Harvard football stadium, and traversing a rock wall and climbing rock and ice every weekend. I easily completed the Boston Marathon in the spring and ran a complete traverse of the Presidential Mountains in New Hampshire in under four hours, normally a three-day hike. When I flew to San Francisco in August 1983 I felt prepared and confident.

An optimistic group gathered in San Francisco. We were going to climb the last unclimbed face on Mount Everest—the hardest mountaineering route that had ever been attempted, and we were going to do it with minimal supplemental oxygen and no native support on the mountain. We traveled through China as a cohesive team. Our collective mentality was similar to what I have read about the psychology of people going off to war. A macabre sense of humor prevailed with lots of "jokes" about climbers who have perished. We all knew that sixty-two lives had already been lost on the slopes of Mount Everest, that no new route had been opened on the mountain without the loss of life, that none had been climbed without native load carriers on the mountain, and that ours was the hardest and most dangerous path. Still, none of us broached the subject of whether an accident could happen to us. Interestingly, there was also a prevalent hypersexuality and much flirtation with stewardesses and other Western sojourners, perhaps our bodies' way of telling us to propagate our gene pool before embarking on the dangerous mission. I personally adopted an attitude that I had trained well enough and was with such a great team that I would be safe. I had no conscious thoughts of the risk. My mind remained completely immersed in the present, with little talk of the past or future, as we again enjoyed banquets and sightseeing.

Arriving in Lhasa I found that Tibet had changed dramatically in two years. The Chinese had eased many of their restrictions. The Potala and Jokang were now crowded with chanting pilgrims, and the streets were bustling with activity. Chinese soldiers were still present, but less obvious. We stayed in a comfortable guest house and ate well. However, there was little time for tourism. We were a team with a mission! We packed our gear on trucks and began the drive to Mount Everest after one day. The monsoon washed out the main road so we took an alternate dirt track that was so bumpy you couldn't even pick your nose. The ride was more beautiful than I remembered. We passed alongside rolling hills with layers of brown, yellow, and green bands woven into the sand. The monsoon gave a constant, unpleasant drizzle; however, the swirling clouds made the landscape all the more impressive. We arrived in Xigatse late in the evening and left for Xegar early the next morning. Despite the hectic pace we were beginning to get to know each other.

It soon became clear to me that my three-hour-per-day training regimen left me one of the weakest members of our team. Three people stood apart as being in a different physical realm. Kim Momb looked like a shorter version of the incredible hulk. He had been high on the West Ridge of Everest the previous spring and trained full time during the intervening two months. Prior to his becoming a professional climber, Kim was a top-ranked skier, motorcross racer, and a blackbelt kickboxer with an undefeated professional record. He had a ready smile and firm handshake. Carl Tobin's income was derived solely from competing as the mountaineer in a made-for-television event called "Survival of the Fittest." One look at his rippled muscular physique and it was easy to see why. He had been living in

Fairbanks and consistently pushing the limits of what had been considered possible in the mountains of Alaska. Carl was quiet with a piercing sense of humor that left one slightly off balance. For instance, when the group discussed romantic movies Carl mumbled earnestly, "Yeah, I always get teary at that love scene in *Deliverance*." When Tibetans stared at Carl, he stared back with a look of such profound, and at the same time simple, curiosity that they turned away. Carl would then follow them, continuing his study. The third powerhouse was Dave Cheesmond, a South African living in Canada. Dave had been Carl's partner on many of his hardest climbs and had distinguished himself as one of the most prolific and accomplished mountaineers in the world during the past two years. "Cheese" was gregarious and helpful and always willing to tip a beer or join in a bawdy song.

A second contingent were the older masters: George Lowe, Lou Reichardt, Andy Harvard, and Chris Kopczynski. George had already established himself as a legendary climber with a will, tenacity, and determination second to none. George had been the driving force on the route in 1981 and exuded a quiet confidence about this trip. Lou, a professor of neurophysiology, had climbed more twenty-six-thousand-foot peaks than any American. He shared George's work ethic. What Lou lacked in technical skills he more than made up for with a physiology that did not seem to be affected by altitude. Andy had been on a phenomenal number of expeditions and was a master of logistics. A lawyer by trade, he was thoughtful and articulate. Chris Kopczynski also knew about expeditions. He reached the top of Everest, via the South Col Route, in 1981 as well as making the first American ascent of the North Face of the Eiger. "Kop" was a building contractor from Spokane, Washington, who had a straightforward Western friendliness and a button with a picture of his wife and kids that he wore over his heart throughout the climb.

I thought of myself as being similar in strength to the other three climbers until we went out for a training run in Beijing. Carlos Buhler, Jay Cassell, and Dave Coombs left me in the dust. Buhler, a mountain guide from Bellingham, Washington, was a full-time climber with wider interests than just mountains. Carlos was multilingual with deep thoughts about international and interpersonal relations. He was warm, but intense, and very sensitive to "feelings" on expeditions. I found Coombs to be an upbeat man who was one of the hardest workers I have ever met. His climbing resume and background were similar to mine. He was a Harvard graduate with an MBA who trained intensively for this trip. Similar in many ways to Coombs was Jay Cassell. Jay was an MBA and ex-marine who had the least big mountain experience on the team. However, he had finished strongly in the Iron Man Triathlon and Western States 100 endurance run, and was, perhaps, our most aerobically fit member. Jay had a personality that was mentally as solid as a rock; he was a man who would break before he bent.

The final two climbers, Morrissey and Dan Reid, were both busy cardiothoracic surgeons in California. Neither was able to spend much time training. In fact, Dan had not climbed since his drug-addled solo ascent of the ropes on Everest in 1981. However, this time he came prepared. Dan had "The Little Engine that Could" embroidered on all of his climbing clothes as well as a formal kilt to wear into base camp. The final member of the team was our "Mister Organization," base camp manager John Boyle. Boyle handled the detail work before the trip and developed a winch system that we hoped would save us considerable time and effort on the mountain. To reach the top of Everest we had a three-part task: We first had to reclimb the sheer initial forty-five-hundred-foot rock and ice buttress. Next, we had to carry enough supplies up the route to support a summit climb. Then, we still had to climb a vertical mile and a half up a steep snow ridge to the top of the world. Boyle's plan was to launch a rocket attached to a cord from the top of the buttress. Next he planned to rig up a continuous nine-thousand-foot loop with high tech yachting pulleys at the top and bottom. He had a Honda engine to power our loads quickly over the difficult climbing. Most of the team was a bit dubious, but we all hoped it would work.

The trek to base camp again started from Kharta. Our gear was loaded onto yaks for the journey. It was a festive march with the colorfully robed Tibetan yak herders whistling, singing, and chanting mantras as we walked. With us on the trek were a group of seven doctor friends of Morrissey's who had donated to the cause and Jack Alustiza, the owner of a Basque restaurant whom Jim had asked to be the expedition base camp chef, our Chinese Liaison Officer who was again Wang Fu Chow and our official interpreter, Mr. Tsao. Boyle, Alustiza, and the scientists were all a bit slower than the climbers, and we adopted a leisurely pace. The views were again stunning with bright red rhododendrons flowering in the monsoon wetness. The mornings were glorious with shimmering peaks dancing above us. By late morning clouds rolled in and covered the sky. Precipitation started before noon every day and lasted until late in the evening. As we gained altitude the rain turned to snow. Dan Reid never wore more than his kilt and stripped naked to bathe in every glacial pond.

We reached base camp at an altitude of seventeen thousand feet at the edge of the Kangshung Glacier on August 26. Everyone, including the scientists, pitched in to get camp set up. The first task was to find and mark the route across the Kangshung Glacier so that we could carry gear to the base of the buttress. I felt the effects of the altitude. My resting pulse raced at over one hundred beats per minute, double my normal rate at sea level. With exertion my pulse pounded in my temples at over two hundred beats per minute. The fourteen-mile-round-trip carry across the glacier to advanced base camp with a heavy pack made for a long, exhausting day. The entire team left early in the morning to make the carry, except for Dan Reid. We passed Dan in the afternoon. He was still a long way from the end of the glacier. We suggested that he dump his load and return with us, but he refused. An hour after dark we were organizing a search party to go out onto the heavily crevassed glacier to look for Dan when we heard him yodel. With a big grin Dr. Reid raved about how beautiful it was to be alone on a glacier at night. Jim and Dan had a talk about risk and danger and Dan agreed to stay in base camp and be good.

On September 1, the actual climb began. Lou, Carl, and I started fixing ropes up the buttress. As the climbing leader from the 1981 trip, Lou had the honor of leading the first pitch of the 1983 effort. The climbing went quickly as we knew exactly where the route should go. We were also helped by several ropes and anchors that were still in place from 1981. We regained seven hundred feet of sheer rock before noon. Dan Reid caught up to us late in the afternoon, carrying more rope. We asked him what he was doing on the route. Reid grinned. "Well, you need more rope, don't you?" Dan soon insinuated himself into the climbing rotation, carrying heavy loads in support of the leaders and helping out everywhere. Once again the crazy doc was a full climbing member of the team.

The lower part of the route climbed up steep rock that had lots of small, sharp, incut holds. We made fast progress, reaching our first campsite on the mountain on the second day. We again called it "Snow Camp," as it sat perched on a magnificent snow ridge at the top of the first rock step. The next obstacle was a difficult ridge of enormous snow mushrooms and steep ice. Dave Cheesmond, Kop, and Coombs moved into the front. I joined Dan in the group carrying equipment up to support the leaders. The first ones up climbed the rock and ice that the mountain offered and fixed a permanent rope in place. The rest of the team used the fixed rope to safeguard themselves and climb with heavy loads. As in 1981, we used mechanical ascenders, which slide up the rope but lock when weighted, to move up, and rappelled back down using figure eight friction rings that slowed our slide down the ropes.

After five days we reached the Bowling Alley, the dangerous ice chute that gives access to the upper face. This gully was still a funnel for debris that melts out of the upper rock headwall and is again one of the scariest sections on the climb. At the top of the Bowling Alley we reestablished "Pinsetter Camp" beneath the rock headwall that was the technically most difficult section of the route. In 1981 it took three weeks to surmount the crumbly, overhanging barrier. Climbing this section required laborious and strenuous aid climbing where the leader pounds a piton into the rock and uses this aid point to advance. Looking up at the path we saw a tattered rope swaying in the breeze, a remnant from the 1981 effort. Kim volunteered to "jug" up the weather-beaten cord. He clipped his mechanical ascenders onto the old rope and methodically began climbing like a spider on a thread. We watched with horror as Kim, a couple of hundred feet above us, hastily detached first one, then the other ascender, and quickly clipped them back on to the rope a few feet higher. In four hours he regained the entire headwall. When I came up, I saw that where Kim detached his ascenders the old rope was worn 95 percent through, so that only one strand of frayed nylon, less than an eighth of an inch in diameter, remained.

I was now supposed to rotate back to advanced base camp for a couple of days of rest while Jay, Andy, Carlos, George, and Cheese moved to the front to push the route up the next section. Above the rock we had to surmount a nine-hundred-foot ice slope angled at seventy degrees that was protected by fifty-foot-high icicles at its top in order to reach the top of the buttress, a place we named the Helmut. Starting down, I met Cheese. He told me that he was not feeling well. He said that he had to turn around and descend back to base camp. Carlos and Andy were also ill. We were short of load carriers. I knew that I was very tired; however, I decided that the team needed me to stay up and work. I was still insecure about my being on this team of great climbers and believed that this was a chance for me to prove my worth. The next morning I carried a fifty-pound load of ropes and ice screws to the top of the rock. Back in the tent at Pinsetter Camp, I was too tired to help Kim with the laborious tasks of melting snow into water and preparing dinner. I crawled into my sleeping bag and began shivering uncontrollably. Kim gave me tea and helped me throughout the night. In the morning I had not slept a minute and was very lethargic. Kim and George helped me pack up and I headed down.

As I started to rappel down the rock below Snow Camp I heard a roar. Looking up I saw that a house-sized block of rock had broken off directly above me. It hit and shattered one hundred feet overhead. Car-sized chunks rained down on me. I curled up as small as possible and realized, "I am going to die." I was calm and my mind was blank as I faced my doom. Three large boulders smashed within five feet of me, but I escaped unscathed. The air was heavy with the acrid, gunpowder-like smell of the rock dust. The sound of the avalanche resonated down the valley. After a moment of calm, my heart began to race. My pulse went over two hundred beats per minute and my whole body shook uncontrollably. It was several minutes before the trembling stopped and I was able to stand and continue my descent.

Jim Morrissey heard of my shivering and lethargy. He was concerned that I had cerebral edema and insisted that I return to base camp for a rest. High altitude cerebral edema, a swelling of the brain, can quickly become fatal. Falling rock can end a climber's life in an instant. Walking dejectedly back across the glacier to base camp, I wondered if climbing any route on any mountain is worth dying for. At the same time I thought about my teammates, realizing that I had never been with a group so full of life. There was an intense prevailing appreciation for both the immense beauty surrounding us and the small joys of existence. I came to help this team climb the Kangshung Face and would return to the cause, if I could. I felt awful that I might have hurt our team's chances for reaching the top, not to mention ruined my own summit aspirations, by pushing myself too hard when I knew that I was not feeling well. I vowed to listen to my body from now on.

The rest of the team quickly succeeded in fixing ropes up to the helmet. The climbing of the buttress has been accomplished in only twelve days. Now we needed to carry our gear up the wall. We all focused on Boyle's winch system. Carlos and Jay carefully uncoiled the polypropylene trail line and aimed the rocket launcher. The first effort dribbled off into an avalanche cone and was lost in the debris. The second firing was also a dud. We only had three rockets. Jim, Lou and Boyle discussed the options. We could hazard another firing from the top station. If it failed we would have no winch support. They decided on a second option, which was to fire a rocket from Snow Camp. The route below was sheer to the glacier. They thought the rocket would surely work from there, and it did. We would get some support from the motorized winch. The second part of the plan was to install a gravity hauling system on the overhanging rock headwall above Pinsetter Camp. Dave Cheesmond and George Lowe engineered a two-thousand-foot continuous line with pulleys at the top and bottom. Haul bags were filled with rock and snow at the top station and clipped onto the rope, while the haul bags filled with our food and equipment were tied on the bottom. The upper haul bags were released and pulled up our gear. Both the gravity system and Boyle's engine-powered winch worked perfectly. We still had to man-carry the loads from Snow Camp up through the Bowling Alley to Pinsetter and from the top of the rock up the steep Helmut ice field. We needed all the manpower we could muster. So, after five days of rest at base camp, I returned to the task. I was feeling much better and hoped that I had a virus and not cerebral edema or any other high altitude illness.

With everyone putting in 110 percent every day, progress moving our gear up the mountain was steady. I again carried as heavy a load as I possibly could, plus ten pounds more every day. The monsoon continued to linger, with wet snow falling every afternoon. Still, everyone of us pushed hard, working with no rest days. We all, of course, had our own summit aspirations, and none of us wanted to burn himself out. Yet, we were in a desperate race against the winter winds and storms. Once the jet stream lowered its one-hundred-mile-per-hour wrath down on the mountain, and the winter Himalayan storms unleashed their fury, it would be impossible for anyone to reach the top. So, despite having already pushed too hard once on the trip, and feeling exhausted at the end of every day, I continued to work with every ounce of my strength. The rest of the team put in an equal effort, which inspired each of us to do more.

Lou, Carl, Carlos, Andy, Dan, Jim, and I were based at Snow Camp, bringing loads up to the gravity winch at Pinsetter Camp, with Lou often making two impossibly heavy carries per day. Jay and Dave Coombs were working the bottom of the gravity winch while George, Cheese, Kim, and Kop dropped down from the Helmut to work the top of the winch and ferry loads back up to the Helmut Camp. Kim put in a herculean effort making two carries every day for a week. We slowly moved more people up as more loads accumulated at the upper winch station. Finally, on September 29 our entire team of thirteen climbers and all of the necessary gear was on top of the buttress.

After a solid month of work we were only at 21,500 feet. This is the same altitude that yaks can walk to on the north side of Everest and where advanced base camp sits in Nepal. We still had a vertical mile and a half to climb on an unknown route and little time before the weather changed for the winter. Statistically, the jetstream lowers during the first two weeks of October. Jim and Lou began to work out a tentative strategy. Everyone had to continue to push as hard and fast as he could. We would establish three higher camps: Camp One at 23,500 feet, Camp Two at 25,500 feet, and Camp Three at nearly 27,000 feet. We had a total of thirteen bottles of supplemental oxygen. So each person would carry his own one bottle of gas up to the high camp, sleep without extra oxygen, and use the bottle of oxygen for the summit climb.

At 21,500 feet I could feel my pulse beating in my temples, even at rest. Every step upward was a new altitude record for me. On October 1, I wrote in my diary:

I realize that I am among the weakest of the thirteen of us. I also know the risks involved, even for the strongest. Consciously, I do not think that it makes sense to jeopardize my life to climb a mountain. But, I am beginning to understand what Mallory must have meant when he said he was climbing Everest "because it is there." It is not just that the mountain is "there" externally, but it is because it is "there" internally, within me. It has become a personal quest. Yes, the beauty of the high mountains, the camaraderie, the teamwork, and the joy of movement are all reasons to be climbing here. But, in these really high mountains there is a definite element of self-realization and of learning exactly where my limits are, driving me upward. I do not want to die. But, this is my shot at the top of the world, and I'm going for it, savoring every moment of life!

The weather turned perfect and the massive team effort continued unabated. By October 5, everyone had been to twenty-five thousand feet without supplemental oxygen. Jim decided that the first summit team would be Kop, George, and Cheese. Along with Lou and Kim they headed up to establish High Camp. The group had to break trail through knee-deep snow angled upward at thirty degrees. With their loads they moved at a pace of four breaths per step with many rests. Digging out a tent platform from the steepening ice at over twenty-seven thousand feet was exhausting. They took turns working until they were gasping, then passed the shovel on to the next climber. It require three hours to chop out space for a single two-man tent. All were too exhausted to stay at the High Camp. Cheese, who had been the strongest and the hardest worker on the team, developed a wet cough at the end of the day. He worried that he might be developing high altitude pulmonary edema and elected to drop back all the way down to Helmut Camp. Kop had a bad headache and decided to descend to Camp One. George felt exhausted and realized that he also could not continue without a rest.

Jim hastily reorganized summit plans. He moved Lou, Kim, and Carlos into the first try. George, Jay, Dan, Kop, and Andy were the new second team. Dave Coombs, Carl, Jim, and I would be the third summit team. It sounded great to me. I could use the extra day of rest that being on the third team would afford. Moreover, with two parties ahead of us we wouldn't have to break trail through deep snow, making it much easier for us. Finally, it was exactly the team I wanted. I liked the concept of a Tabin-Tobin summit team. Carl's razor-sharp wit, laid-back personality, and incredible strength made him a joy to climb with. Dave Coombs was as mentally tough as anyone I've ever met and the most safety-conscious member of our team, which is a great asset for an Everest summit partner. Jim was a person I admired greatly with whom I would be honored to share the big day.

The plan was to rotate the three teams to the top in three days. We had two tents at twenty-five thousand feet and a two-man tent at High Camp. You can descend quickly from the High Camp to Camp Two by sliding on your butt in the snow, breaking with an ice axe. The first team would go to High Camp, sleep without supplemental oxygen, and use their bottles to go for the top. They would then descend to the second camp where the third team would have hot drinks waiting for them. Meanwhile, the second team would have moved to High Camp. The next day, team two would summit and descend to Camp Two where the first team would take care of them. Meanwhile, the final team would move into position for a summit bid. On the third day my group would climb to the top of Mount Everest and descend as far as possible. An air of excitement engulfed us. In three days we would have either made it or failed.

On October 8, Carlos, Kim, and Lou set out for the summit of Mount Everest at two o'clock in the morning. George, Dan, Andy, Kop, and Jay headed for High Camp. Jim, Carl, Dave Coombs, and I set off for Camp Two. The first big news was that Andy had a sharp pain in his chest and a deep cough. Jim's diagnosis was an inflammation of the lining of the lungs. Andy headed down to base camp. Jim decided that as a doctor he had to stay with Andy and turned around. Next, Carl found that his toes were freezing and he could not warm them. He had developed frostbite in Alaska the previous winter and decided that the summit of Everest was not worth the risk for him, as he would surely lose his toes and the frozen foot would add to the danger of a fall. Next, Coombs developed a terrible headache and was unable to hold down food. Worried that he was developing cerebral edema, he turned back.

My entire summit team had disintegrated on me. We all returned to Camp One. I was very upset and confused as to what to do. I felt good enough to go for the summit, but was afraid to try it alone. Then, Cheese called on the radio to say that he was feeling healthy again and was keen to make a bid. Dave Cheesmond and I thus became the new third team. We planned to move to Camp Two, at twenty-five thousand feet, the next day. Meanwhile, the weather remained perfect with a cloudless calm sky. Jay, Dan, and George reached High Camp feeling strong. We all eagerly awaited word from the first summit team. The second team reported that the snow was deep above camp. Trail breaking must have been exhausting for Kim, Carlos, and Lou.

At noon we got an excited radio call from our Chinese interpreter, Mr. Tsao, who was watching the progress from base camp via a high-powered telescope. "I see climbers on ridge! Climbers are on ridge!" he reported. This was at 28,000 feet where our route merged with the Southeast Ridge. The East Face had been climbed! Now we only needed to follow the ridge to the top. In the background on the radio we heard Tibetans chanting mantras for our success. The next message we heard was bizarre. "Seven climbers, seven climbers going to get them!" We had no idea what Tsao was talking about. We later learned that a Japanese team climbing the South Col route from Nepal met up with our team just below the South Summit at 28,500 feet. The Japanese were climbing without supplemental oxygen and soon fell behind our climbers.

The final climb to the South Summit was steeper and scarier than expected. The angle was over forty-five degrees with a hard crust over sugar snow. It would have been impossible to self-arrest a fall. To save time and weight they were climbing unroped. Any slip would be fatal. Above the South Summit a heavily corniced knife-edged ridge lead to the short vertical obstacle known as the "Hillary Step." This thirty-foot wall was passed by strenuously bridging one foot on rock while kicking the other foot's crampon points into the ice. Finally, at two-thirty in the afternoon, twelve hours after starting out from High Camp, Kim's voice crackled on the radio, "We're on top of this fucker!"

Back at Camp One we whooped with joy and hugged all around. Kim, Carlos, and Lou walked the final steps to the top together. Kim was openly weeping on the top of the world. The three spent forty-five minutes in perfect sunshine and air calm enough to light a candle, enjoying the view and taking photographs. All three were out of supplemental oxygen when they cautiously headed down. They encountered the Japanese, still stumbling upward, at the South Summit. None of them had a pack. This meant that they did not have any extra clothing, sleeping bags, water, or stoves for a bivouac. It was past four o'clock in the afternoon. Our team suggested that it was too late and that the Japanese should turn around. They shook their noticeably blue faces and continued upward. A Sherpa climbing with the Japanese then fell and started sliding ten feet above them. Lou looked directly into the terrified man's eyes as he tumbled past, missing Lou by only a few inches, before accelerating into a seven-thousand-foot drop into the Western Cwm. A few minutes later one of Lou's footholds gave way and he flipped upside down, suspended by only one foot punched through the hard crust in the snow. He hung, unable to right himself, with just a couple of toes keeping him from falling off the mountain. If his foot had let go he would have torpedoed seven thousand feet, head first, following the path of the Sherpa to certain death. Carlos climbed fifteen feet back up to help him. Badly shaken by the near fall and having watched the Sherpa perish, Lou and Carlos faced into the slope and backed slowly down the steep ice.

Kim continued descending alone, unaware of Lou's slip and reached High Camp at six o'clock. He came down all the way to Camp One, joining me in my tent at 23,500 feet at eight o'clock. I had never seen a human being who looked as exhausted as Kim. His eyes were sunk back into his face and he was barely able to whisper. Meanwhile, Carlos and Lou still had not returned to high camp. Our team became progressively more anxious. Kim postulated that they may have opted to descend the easier route down to the South Col in Nepal and stay with the Japanese. We worried that they had fallen. Finally, at nine o'clock, George reported that they had staggered into High Camp. Six people were crammed into the tiny two-person tent, so that any movement by one person affected everyone else. Lou had terrible nightmares and coughed incessantly. Carlos had full-body muscle cramps and convulsions. No one got any sleep. Dan later said that, physically, the hardest part of his summit day was holding Carlos' arms and legs during the night.

At two o'clock in the morning, on October 9, George started brewing up, melting snow into water. At three-thirty he was set to go. Kopczynski had had a bad headache all night and felt it was getting worse. He was also concerned about Lou and Carlos going down alone. Kop volunteered to help them. Dan and Jay wavered a bit, then decided to go for the summit. Since the track had partially blown in, they decided that George should start out breaking trail and they would catch up. The wind picked up toward morning. After an hour George stopped and looked back. He saw no one behind him. He later wrote in his diary:

Wind whips snow across my face. Can't even tell if I'm standing up straight. Complete vertigo! So alone! Have never felt such an alien environment, clearly a place where man was not meant to be. Why haven't Jay and Dan started? Storm is increasing—will just continue 'til it seems unreasonable.

Dan and Jay discussed what to do for a long time. When they finally decided to go for it, Dan found that the oxygen fogged his glasses, and they were delayed further as Dan struggled to clear his vision. Meanwhile, down at Camp One, I brewed up for Kim and enjoyed a celebratory breakfast of tinned cake and pudding. Jim Morrissey came over to our tent. He was elated at the team's success and said he now just wanted to see everyone safely off of the mountain. Cheese joined us in great spirits, totally optimistic about our summit bid. "The track will be in so we'll just walk up the steps. We'll have a perfect summit day, Geoff," he said. I was feeling great and was very happy to have Dave as my summit partner. We headed up to the next camp carrying our oxygen bottles and personal gear. At Camp Two we had a great reunion with Lou and Carlos coming down.

Both were wasted, but healthy. Kop was also feeling better. His headache was gone and he opted to join me and Cheese and go back up. This increased my confidence. Not only was Kop strong and safe, but he'd been to the top before. I only wished that Jim, who had also been powerful and fit, had decided to join us.

The wind increased in intensity as the morning wore on. Clouds began to build down in the valley and move up the mountain. Up high, George was continuing to climb solo and he was finding very hard snow and a steeper slope than he expected. He climbed cautiously as he knew that he could not self-arrest a fall. Then, he saw a figure above. In his diary he wrote, "He moves incredibly slowly, taking a few steps, then collapsing on his ice axe to rest. I am going up and he is coming down. Yet, we are covering ground at about the same rate. I ask the Japanese climber if he is okay. He replies, 'bivy,' and points up. He is very blue and his motions uncoordinated. I have no rope to help him, so just pat him on the shoulder and continue."

Dan and Jay were now struggling up the lower slopes finding that George's steps had already disappeared with the wind. Cheese, Kop, and I watched the weather carefully. Dave reassured me that the clouds were just down in the valley and conditions should hold a few more days. I still worried about my own summit chances as I watched the mist slowly creep up the mountain.

The climbing steepened for George. Just below the South Summit he turned up the rate of his oxygen flow. At the South Summit he found a movie camera left by a Japanese climber the day before and he wondered how many had to bivouac. George moved onto the dramatic upper ridge and over the Hillary Step. He continued in his diary:

Above the Hillary section is a steep bulge of snow. It feels awkward moving over it, especially since I can't see well with the mask and goggles. Immediately above is an ice axe sticking in the snow. Looking down I see scrape marks in the snow until they end at steep rock a few meters below. The realization hits that one of the Japanese died here yesterday. I push on, now just wanting to be finished.

George reached the summit just before ten o'clock in the morning. He spent a half hour surveying the view, turned up his oxygen, and started the descent. He picked up the Japanese ice axe for added security on the steep sections. At noon he met Jay and Dan just below the dangerous part. George told them about the Japanese and urged them to set a turnaround time. He recalled, "Dan says they will turn around by one-thirty. Knowing Dan does not give me any confidence in that prediction."

George stopped briefly at our top tent and left his extra oxygen. He also turned on his headlamp and left it suspended from the top of the tent in case Dan and Jay returned after dark. He then zipped down, stopping for a quick congratulatory hug and a brew at our camp, and reached Helmut Camp by four o'clock in the afternoon. I was very psyched by George's fast ascent. Our team had already achieved great success, and I began to believe that I would reach the top of Everest. During the next two hours the clouds continued to surge up the mountain and the wind began to whip the tent. I began to worry about my summit chances. George's footprints were already invisible outside our tent. Then the realization hit: Dan and Jay were still out there! The storm intensified into a white out blizzard as the sun set. "Death-pact PercoDan" had not been on a mountain in two years. This was Jay's first trip to the Himalayas. Worry gave way to panic, made all the worse because there was nothing we could do. It would be impossible for anyone to survive a night out at this altitude, in this storm. Then, at nine o'clock, Dan and Jay came on the radio to say they had just returned to the High Camp tent.

They, of course, had ignored the turnaround time. Jay and Dan reached the summit at three-fifteen, out of supplemental oxygen. They stayed on top until four o'clock and started to descend, just as the storm hit them. For psychological support they took a small length of rope that Dan had carried and tied themselves together so that if one fell they both would die. Both were totally exhausted and disoriented in the blizzard. It was completely dark. Both were freezing. At eight o'clock they argued about where to go. Dan felt that they must have passed the tent and advocated going back up. Jay was too tired to ascend and insisted they must have lost the ridge and that they should move laterally. Then, the storm abated for an instant and they saw a glimmer of a light beneath them. An hour of desperate struggle later they found the High Camp tent and crawled inside. George's headlamp battery had gone dead, but it lasted just long enough to help Jay and Dan survive.

Dawn on October 10 revealed the full fury of the mountain. The blizzard still raged. High winds and two feet of new, wind-blown snow made it difficult to move, and the avalanche danger was extreme. There was no question. We had to go down. Kop, Cheese, and I waited for Dan and Jay, then begin breaking trail down to Helmut Camp. Jay's right hand had fingers black with frostbite, but he never complained. Dan was having visual problems from his glasses becoming covered with snow, but he kept on smiling, even after he wandered off the trail and tumbled twenty feet, stopping only a few inches from a fatal drop. I descended down the avalanche chute, tied Dan to a rope, and helped him out. We crawled, wet and miserable, into Helmut Camp after seven hours of hard work. The next day we rappelled down into the swirling tempest, having to dig out icy ropes which had frozen into the buttress. Forty scary times we slid down the slick ropes with freezing hands barely able to work the braking device. We were trying to bring all of our gear and garbage off of the mountain with us and it was difficult to balance the enormous loads. At the top of the Bowling Alley I slipped and my pack flipped me upside down. Spindrift avalanches swept over me. I couldn't breathe and couldn't untangle myself. Just as I start to drown, Dr. Dan returned my favor of the previous day and came back up a rope to save my life.

Eight hours later our entire team was reunited at advanced base camp. Everyone was safe. With the exception of Jay, who would lose a couple of fingertips to frostbite, all of us were healthy. Six Americans reached the top of Mount Everest via the first ascent of the largest, steepest, and most difficult face on the mountain. We did it with a minimum of supplemental oxygen and no native support or porters on the climb. More importantly, we did it as a team of brothers who were all leaving the mountain as friends, bonded for life.

Pushing the Edge

FOR ME, THE ASCENT of the East Face of Mount Everest was an experience of maximal intensity, and totally fulfilling. I had not personally made the top, but felt good about my effort toward the team's success. Still, I could not help but wonder whether, if the weather had cooperated, I would have been able to make it to the summit. I was not as strong as several of my teammates who nearly died going to the top. I had pushed hard, but not to the very edge of my limits. I wanted to know exactly what I was capable of. During the next two years I continued to expand my limits on technically difficult rock and ice climbs. Reaching the top of a climb was not the issue, it was maximizing my efforts during every moment. This philosophy also extended into my academic efforts.

I graduated from Harvard Medical School in the spring of 1985 and immediately went to Nepal. With me were Steve Ruoss, my main climbing partner in Boston during the past year, Jim Traverso, a climbing guide who was living in Katmandu, and Dave Dossetter, an old friend who was new to climbing and would trek with us. We were joined by a young Sherpa named Dawa Tsering whom Jim arranged to have as our trekking guide. Dawa Tsering and I quickly became good friends despite having no language in common. He told me that he wanted to be a climber. We joked about climbing Mount Everest together. Little did either of us suspect that three years later we would embrace on top of the world.

Our plan for the pre-monsoon season of 1985 was to walk through the Khumbu region near Mount Everest to acclimatize,

and then climb two twenty-one-thousand-foot peaks by technically difficult routes. Trekking through the Nepal Himalayas in
the spring is one of the most pleasurable activities I know. There
are no roads, only hiking paths, connecting the villages. The
native people maintain these routes of transportation and com-
merce such that the walking surface is usually perfect. Yaks carry
all of the heavy gear. We walked unencumbered, with only a
light day pack on our backs. The spring days were long and
sunny with green budding in the forests, alpine flowers bloom-
ing bright orange, violet, pink, and red near our feet and the
snow-covered peaks dancing in the deep blue sky above. The
pungent smell of rhododendron, juniper, and pine tickled our
noses in the crisp clear air. Our Sherpa cook boy started every
day with a smile and, "Chai Sahib, Geoff," bringing sweet Sherpa milk tea to my tent. Next came a four-course breakfast. We
walked leisurely, taking in the views, for several hours each
morning and afternoon with a long break for a sumptuous lunch
in a scenic location every afternoon. The trail was dotted with
Sherpa tea houses. These smoky wooden structures were the
source of lots of laughter, *chai*, and home-brewed "chang."
Being part of a small group with an equal number of Americans
and Sherpas, we were welcomed into many homes and parties.
We spent two weeks wandering and adapting to the altitude.

All five of us then walked up to the easily accessible eighteen-
thousand-foot summit of Gokyo Ri, from where many of the
best pictures of Mount Everest have been taken. From the top
we could survey five of the world's eight highest mountains.
Next, Jim and I climbed a beautiful, steep snow ridge to the
twenty-one-thousand-foot summit of Parcharmo. It was impossible to set anchors in the ridge, so we moved together with the
knowledge that if one of us fell, the other would have to immediately jump off the other side of the ridge. Parcharmo bridges
the Rawaling region and the Khumbu. The 360-degree panora-
ma from its top spans the seemingly endless Tibetan plateau on
one side and the lush terraced rice paddy fields glowing green
beneath us in Nepal. However, our main goal was for Steve, Jim,
and I to climb the sheer seven-thousand-foot North Face of

Kusum Kangruru. This would be the first ascent of the steepest line on one of the most difficult mountains in Nepal.

A storm blasted us and the mountain while we were on the final approach walk to the peak, coating everything with wet snow. From our base camp at fourteen thousand feet we surveyed the vertical mile-and-a-half wall above us. The North Face proper was too dangerous from the threat of avalanches, so we switched our objective to an unexplored rock buttress on the Northeast Ridge of Kusum Kangruru. We estimated that the climb would take five days up and down. With this in mind we brought food for four days and fuel to melt snow into water for six days. The trek and previous ascents allowed us to become well acclimatized. Our plan was to climb the route "alpine style," starting at the bottom and climbing to the top with no fixed ropes or permanent camps on the mountain. The climbing started on steep rock that was continually challenging, but never desperate. We anchored to tiny ledges to spend the nights. We had to carry food, fuel, climbing gear, and clothes for the ascent and our packs weighed over fifty pounds. I attempted to reduce the size of my load by leaving my sleeping bag behind. I tried to sleep in a down suit and bivouac sack, but found I was too cold. I shivered and watched the stars until dawn every night. We made steady progress up the cliff. However, rime ice coated the stone and every move was tenuous. The difficulty required removing our gloves to hang on tiny edges, but then our fingers would quickly go numb. It took us six days to surmount the five thousand vertical feet of rock climbing. By this time we had been out of food for more than a day and we had no more fuel to melt snow into water. Above us a snow ridge led to the summit, only seven hundred feet higher in altitude. We chopped sleeping platforms out of the ice for our seventh night on the mountain. My mouth felt like I had swallowed glue. The next day I could barely swallow and my throat felt like a heard of yaks had stampeded through during the long night. Still, we started for the peak at first light. The ridge had a double cornice, and we had to anchor and belay each rope length of progress. At one o'clock in the afternoon we were still a few hours from the top. We

were past all the difficulties. The summit looked close enough
to touch. However, we had been climbing above twenty thousand feet for twenty-four hours without water and nearly three
days without food. Any exertion caused panting and we lost
more moisture with every breath. It was now a struggle just to
remain standing. Steve looked at me and asked, "What do you
think, man?"

"I'm wasted," I whispered. Jim stood behind me and nodded.

"It's down or die!" Steve concluded.

With no further discussion we belayed back down the corniced ridge and started retreating down the wall. The rock was
too difficult to climb down, so we placed anchors and rappelled.
We tied our two ropes together with the knot near the anchor,
slid down the doubled rope, then pulled one end to retrieve the
ropes. On our third rappel a rock was dislodged and cut one rope
near its middle. Now, instead of dropping 165 feet each time, we
were only able to descend less than 100 feet from each anchor.
Two rappels later a second rock cut our other rope. Now we
were reduced to 75-foot rappels. This meant we were both
descending more slowly and running out of equipment to secure
our ropes. Moreover, the rock was loose and it was difficult to
find safe anchors. We continued our desperate retreat through
the night. Loose rocks pelted down around us, whistling past,
sounding like missiles in the dark. We were all beyond exhaustion and moving purely by instinct. I had no conscious thoughts;
there was no conversation; all energy was focussed on the task.
Still, we worked perfectly as a team, communicating silently. If
any of us made a mistake in placing an anchor all three would
die. Our bodies screamed for us to stop, sit, and rest, but we
knew that if we did we would never get up. Thirty-six hours of
maximal concentration later we safely reached the glacier. Steve's
fingers were swollen like sausages and his face was puffed up like
a blowfish. My tongue had expanded to the point where it completely filled my mouth and I was unable to swallow or talk. But,
we were alive! I had learned how much reserve strength I could
muster when all bridges were out behind me and there was
nowhere to go but on.

This experience stood me in good shape for an every-other-night-on-call surgical internship at the University of Colorado. I actually enjoyed the year. My learning curve was very steep and there was great satisfaction for me in gaining competence as a physician. It was also a wonderful climbing year for me. Henry Lester was living in Boulder and specializing in short, severe, overhanging, rock test pieces requiring maximal gymnastics, and we renewed our partnership. In addition, George Lowe was living in Denver. George pushed me to maximize my time off, accepting no excuses. During a period when I worked twelve-hour shifts in the emergency ward, George helped me take advantage of a rare twenty-four hours of freedom to climb a route on the Diamond Wall of Long's Peak in Rocky Mountain National Park. I worked until midnight and had to be back in the emergency room at midnight the next day. George picked me up at the hospital. I slept in the car until we arrived at the parking lot at the base of Long's Peak at three o'clock in the morning. We hiked to the base of the climb at eight, finished twelve pitches of rock climbing by four in the afternoon, scrambled to the top of the mountain, and descended to George's car by nine. I napped in the car and returned to work at midnight, surviving my shift without a mistake or mishap.

A thirty-two-hour break was enough to climb a six-hundred-foot sandstone spire called "Moses Tower" in Canyonlands National Park with George and Neal Beidleman thanks to George's pilot's license. A week's vacation allowed me to climb a five-day route up the overhanging three-thousand-foot granite face of El Capitan in Yosemite Valley with Tom Dickey. I particularly enjoy the sensation of big wall life, hanging progressively higher each night, and watching the everyday world below, and its problems, becoming smaller and smaller.

In 1986 I began a residency in orthopedic surgery in Chicago. I enjoyed the work and the city, but missed the mountains. With Matthew Childs, Rob Slater, Arturo Perez-Reyes, Mike McCarron, and Brad Werntz, I lived the life of a climber in exile. The six of us "buildered" together, climbing on the walls of buildings, and made the long drive to climb at Devil's Lake, Wisconsin. My girlfriend, Beth Peterson, was in Denver and, for the first time in my life, I found myself wishing I were someplace else. In December of 1987, Jim Frush, a climber I spent time with in Nepal in 1985, called from Seattle and invited me to come as a doctor on his Mount Everest expedition the next year. Everyone that I mentioned the trip to said the same thing: "Impossible! You cannot quit a residency in orthopedic surgery!" I did not hesitate. I told Jim, "Yes!"

It was five years since the ascent of the East Face of Everest. The mountain was still "there" inside of me. In addition to the expeditions to Tibet and the Nepal trip in 1985, I had been climbing in the Andes three times. I knew my body and what I needed to do to climb Mount Everest. I returned to sprinting stadium steps while I was in Chicago. When I finished my commitment to my residency in June, I moved to Colorado to train full time for six weeks. I was going on the expedition as a doctor with a first priority of keeping everyone on my team healthy. But, in the spirit of Dr. Dan Reid, I was ready to take the risks to reach the top of the world. What I was not prepared for, however, was the craziness I encountered on Mount Everest in 1988.

Heavy Traffic on the Everest Highway 1988

THE RIDGE I AM CLIMBING is barely two feet wide. To the east is a sheer drop of twelve thousand feet into Tibet. Westward it is eight thousand feet down to the next landing, in Nepal. The angle increases from seventy degrees to vertical at the Hillary Step. Climbing unroped, I delicately balance the crampon points on my right foot on an edge of rock. I swing my left foot, with all my remaining strength, into the adjoining ice. Precariously balanced on quarter-inch spikes attached to my boots, I gasp for breath. Forty feet higher the angle eases. Adrenaline mixed with joy surges through me. After eight hours of intense concentration, I know I will make it. The seventy-mile-an-hour wind threatens to blow me off the ridge. The ambient temperature is far below zero. Yet, I feel flushed with warmth. Ahead stretches a five-foot-wide walkway angled upward at less than ten degrees. Thirty minutes later, just after ten o'clock in the morning, the path ends in a platform of ice the size of a small desk. Everything is below me. I am the two hundred and ninth person to stand on the summit of Mount Everest.

The sky is deep blue and cloudless. The cliché is true, the vistas do seem to stretch infinitely in all directions. I look down over Lhotse, the world's fourth highest peak, upon the endless chain of mountains in Nepal. The Tibetan plateau on the other side extends to the horizon, where I can see the curve of the world dropping away. For fifteen minutes I savor the view as the highest person on earth. Then the crowds start to arrive.

Within an hour climbers from three countries are taking turns being photographed on the summit of Mount Everest. An

American woman arrives on top. A Korean makes the climb solo to commemorate the October 2 closing ceremony of the Seoul Olympics. On the way down the woman, Peggy Luce, becomes snow-blind and then takes a near fatal fall before being rescued by the heroism of Dawa Tsering Sherpa. And this is one of the dullest days of the season.

Thirteen teams from ten countries made at least one attempt on every face and ridge on Mount Everest during the post-monsoon season of 1988. It was the first time that the Nepalese and Chinese gave out multiple permits for a mountain. Climbing styles ranged from siege tactics utilizing fixed camps, Sherpa porters, and supplemental oxygen to a solo, oxygenless, nonstop attempt from base camp. Everyone was out to set a record or do something new. Without a "first" it is nearly impossible to obtain sponsorship.

I was with the Northwest American Everest Expedition. Our team of eleven climbers, led by Seattle attorney Jim Frush, included three women bidding to become the first American woman to climb Mount Everest. The media played up this angle, as did our sponsors. Having been there before gave me a realistic perspective on the task ahead. Any success would have to be a team effort. Diana Dailey, Peggy Luce, and Stacy Allison were all selected for their climbing ability, strength, and personal qualities. They just happened to be women. On the mountain we would all be equal.

Chomolungma treats everyone equally. The Sherpa people and Tibetans, who live in her shadow, call the Goddess Mother of the Earth Chomolungma. They believe she resides in the mountain bearing her name. In 1842 the British survey of India calculated the height of Chomolungma to be 29,002 feet above sea level (it is actually 29,028 by modern measurements), and proclaimed it the highest mountain in the world. In 1863 the English renamed her Mount Everest, after Sir George Everest, a former Surveyor General of India, and proposed that she should be climbed. They brought Sherpa people along on their initial foray and were amazed by their strength at altitude and natural mountaineering talent. Moreover, as ardent followers of

Mahayana Buddhism who believe that true Nirvana should be delayed until everyone on earth finds happiness, they are a delight to be with. They have accompanied so many expeditions that the name "Sherpa" has become synonymous with the job of high-altitude porter. Thirty Sherpas accompanied our expedition.

On August first we left Katmandu for the twenty-day approach march to the mountain. Trekking in the Himalayas can be inspiring. But the only poem to result from our muddy monsoon walk through the torrential rain was titled "Leech On My Dingus." There are two windows of less terrible weather in the Himalayas: one immediately before and one just after the monsoon. During the long winter the one-hundred-mile-an-hour jetstream winds lower to twenty-three thousand feet. Daily monsoon snows limit visibility and create prohibitive avalanche danger during the summer. We were suffering now, hoping to take advantage of a post-monsoon window of good weather on the mountain.

The Sherpas know the suffering Chomolungma can cause. Ninety-six people have died on her slopes. Before going to Everest we had to go to the Thangboche Monastery for a *Pujah*, or blessing ceremony, for safety on the climb. Set on a ridge crest directly below the spectacular summit of Ama Dablam and ringed by Everest, Nuptse, Lhotse and Thamserku, Thangboche is a place where prayers will reach the Gods. Twenty monks chanted continuously for twenty-four hours while the pungent smell of rancid yak butter mixed with the aroma of incense and burning juniper branches. Six monks worked for five days creating an intricate sand painting beseeching Chomolungma to be kind, and we had personal blessings from the Rimpoche Lama.

The Rimpoche Lama of Thangboche is the highest reincarnation in the region. The Sherpas believe that he founded the monastery four reincarnations ago and that he has mystical powers. When the Rimpoche dies they search the countryside for his reborn form. The current Rimpoche Lama is a wizened man of about sixty with laughing eyes shining from an otherwise impassive calm face. He personally said prayers for my safety and tied a blessed red "protection cord" around my neck. I hoped that they picked the right guy.

Three nights later I had my doubts. At four-thirty in the morning the world began to shake and vibrate. It was impossible to stand up on the moving tilt-a-whirl that had been the ground. Then, as the shaking stopped the thunderous roar of avalanches filled the pitch-black air. We later learned that the earthquake registered 6.9 on the Richter scale and killed over two thousand people. Geologically we were in an unstable area. The Himalayas are being formed from the movement of tectonic plates. The Indian Subcontinent crashed into Eurasia twenty million years ago causing a subduction zone of uplift, the highest point of which is Mount Everest. India is still moving at a speed of three centimeters per year relative to Eurasia, so the Himalayas are still being uplifted. We were lucky the earthquake struck when it did. Had it come two weeks later, when we were climbing, we would have been killed. Instead it shook down most of the unstable snow and ice that accumulated during the monsoon, making the mountain safer.

Finally, on August 24 we walked out of the rain into the snow of base camp at 17,500 feet on the Khumbu Glacier. The setting was on jumbled glacial moraine at the end of a long valley with the majestic peaks of Nuptse, Pumori, and the West Shoulder of Everest towering over us. The only gaps in the boxed-in canyon were back down the glacier or up the Khumbu Icefall ahead. The Nepalese call the Khumbu Icefall the "jaws of death." We would have to pass this obstacle to gain the upper slopes of the mountain. First we had to turn the glacier into our home for two months. Garbage from past expeditions was strewn about and had to be cleaned up. Ironically, much of the debris had "Everest Cleanup Expedition" stamped on it. It took a week to flatten platforms for tents, build shelters of stone walls covered with tarps for cooking and communal dining, and unpack equipment. I felt fine when I arrived at base camp, but panted for breath after chopping at the ice for one minute. The seven days spent preparing camp were good for acclimatization and I felt ready to go.

First we had to have one more *Pujah* to consecrate the stone altar our Sherpas built in the center of camp. They erected a flagpole with hundreds of colorful prayer flags extending in a triangle out over the glacier from the top, believing that the wind would carry their prayers to the gods. Offerings of food and liquor were made. The High Lama of the Pangboche Monastery and three other monks came up to chant, juniper was burned, and blessed rice and *tsampa*, a barley flour that is a staple of the Sherpa diet, were tossed into the air. Next all of the alcohol was consumed and a drunken food fight erupted. Sherpas and sahibs were covered in tsampa staggering around the glacier. We decided to acclimatize for one more day.

At three o'clock in the morning on September 1, I started into the Khumbu Icefall. A river of ice flows from the upper slopes of Everest and Lhotse down through a flat valley known as the Western Cwm. The angle changes abruptly with the ice tumbling steeply for two thousand vertical feet to the Khumbu Glacier, forming the icefall. It is an area where unstable ice formations the size of apartment buildings frequently and unpredictably crash down amidst ever-changing crevasses. Dozens of climbers have been crushed to death attempting to negotiate its jaws. In addition, five-thousand-foot walls of ice rise on either side threatening to erase any path that we attempted. If it weren't Everest I would not risk the objective danger, but, it is and I will.

A large Korean team moved in next to us at base camp. They had a permit for the South Pillar route which also starts with the icefall. We worked together to fix the route. This involved finding the least dangerous path and then placing a safety rope, anchored into the ice, to use when climbing with a heavy load. There were numerous crevasses, or cracks, in the ice. Looking down into the gaping holes I could see for hundreds of feet without discerning a bottom. But the scary ones are those you can't see because their openings are covered with fresh snow. To protect ourselves while establishing the route one person was always anchored into the ice playing out the rope, ready to catch the leader should he fall. After climbing the pitch (about 150 feet) the leader secured himself and belayed up the second. This is standard technique unless you are climbing with the mighty and dangerous Om.

The "most dangerous man in Korea" stands five-feet-five-inches tall, has enormous hydraulic pistons for legs, and a never-ending mischievous grin. Hong Gil Om has a fifth degree black-belt in Tae Kwon Do, a second degree blackbelt in Ju Jitsu, and is a member of Korea's elite antiterrorist squad specializing in underwater demolition. In 1987 he reached twenty-eight thousand feet on Everest during the winter. We were paired together leading in the icefall. I went one rope length, anchored myself to the ice, and belayed Om up to me. He led the next section, disappearing over an ice cliff. A few minutes later the rope tugged at my harness. Assuming Om was anchored, I began to climb. The rope pulled a substantial portion of my weight as I balanced upward on the front points of the metal crampons attached to my boots. Climbing vertical ice is strenuous, particularly at twenty thousand feet, and I appreciated the tight rope from above. Surmounting the final overhanging bulge I stepped into deep snow angled upward at forty degrees. I was promptly pulled over, planting my face in the snow. Standing up, I struggled to where the rope went up another ice serac. On top of this obstacle, gasping for breath, I realized I had been following this "pitch" for three hundred feet. Then, the rope yanked me over again. Ahead was Om, his legs churning madly in the thigh-deep snow, with an ice axe in one hand and an upside down ski pole in the other. I yelled for him to stop, but he just laughed and continued to tow me, like a water-skier, up the mountain.

Om led 80 percent of the route we shared with the Koreans. He was not a safe climber by American standards, but in the Himalayas speed can mean safety and success. With his help we reached Camp Two on September 5, six days ahead of schedule. A few of us had been affectionately referring to the Koreans as "the dogeaters" behind their backs. I decided to find out if Om was powered by dogmeat. Sharing a mug of Ginseng tea on hard blue ice angled at seven degrees at 21,600 feet, I asked Om if he ate dog. He spoke little English, but after three minutes of pantomime and barking, Om understood the question. He shook his head saying, "No like, No like." I then raised the question of whether he had sex with animals. Whirling through the air his left leg rocketed out, propelling my teacup fifty feet, his right boot tapped my nose, and Om landed gently on the ice without spilling a drop of his own tea. I assume he meant no.

A greater danger than teasing Om remained the Khumbu Icefall. After establishing the route we still had to carry food and equipment up the mountain. Nearly two hundred loads needed to be carried through the icefall. The glacier shifts constantly, necessitating daily repairs to keep the path open. Worse, the threat of an ice cliff toppling over on us was always present. We climbed during the dark, as fast as possible, because the warmth of the sunlight makes unstable areas more likely to break off. At 5:30 A.M. on September 3, I was in the area where four climbers were killed during the 1982 Canadian Everest Expedition, crossing the detritus from a previous avalanche, when I heard a loud crack. A massive ice cliff broke loose from the West Shoulder of Everest, four thousand feet above me, scraping the rock clean for a horizontal quarter mile.

I was next to Mr. Chung, a powerful Korean climber. Don Goodman, the rock solid deputy leader of my expedition, and Kami Phurba Sherpa were just above us. We desperately looked for somewhere to go as the white death increased in size and in its seeming intent to bear down directly upon us. Alas, as Joe Louis said, there was "no place to run, no place to hide." Feeling as secure as if I were locked in a rolling boxcar with a starved three-hundred-pound sewer rat, I squeezed into a crevasse, secured myself to the fixed line, drove my ice axe in to the hilt and waited. I glanced over at Mr. Chung who was similarly anchored and said, trying to reassure myself, "I think it will stop."

He returned a weak smile and said, "I hope!"

The avalanche floated down in slow motion as if Sam Peckinpah were directing it to maximize my anxiety. Don Goodman recalls thinking, "So this is what it is like to die in the Khumbu Icefall." My terror lessened slightly upon seeing a large cloud of snow billowing up and out toward me. Generally the avalanche itself moves much faster than the cloud of snow and wind that follows. I was waiting to feel the windblast that would indicate survival when a wall of ice slammed into me. I heard a cry from my right side, but I was blasted about the head and shoulders and could not see Mr. Chung being swept away. It felt like twenty lightweight contenders were using my body as a speedbag, simultaneously, without gloves. I pressed down, trying to cover my head with my pack and arms and my mind went blank. The pummeling gave way to a swirling gale-force wind with crystals of ice choking my lungs. Then, all was quiet. I was surprised that I could move all four limbs. I lifted my head. Everything was white. Mr. Chung, Don, and Kami Phurba had vanished.

I ran down the avalanche's path screaming, "Hello! Don! Chung! I'm here to dig you out! Hello!" Thirty seconds later Mr. Chung, looking like a dazed snowman, emerged slowly from a crevasse. He had been swept three hundred feet and, like me, escaped with only bruises. A minute later we found Don Goodman tending to a stunned Kami Phurba. They had been pushed over a thirty-foot ice cliff and miraculously escaped being buried. We were lucky . Had the avalanche been 1 percent bigger or had we been fifty feet higher we'd be dead. It was typical of Don Goodman to be more concerned with everyone else when he had the most severe injuries. Don's right hand was deformed by a broken bone. He barely flinched when I reset it for him. We limped back to base camp to find another kind of tempest building.

Czechoslovakian, New Zealand, and French Mount Everest Expeditions had arrived at base camp and were told that they would have to pay to use our path through the icefall. Jim Frush and the Korean leader, Mr. Nam, worked out the equipment and transportation costs of establishing the route. They decided that this cost should be shared equally by all teams using the ropes. Frush, a successful attorney, had a compelling case. Our route was clearly the safest, and none of the other teams had brought enough equipment to fix a new route. So, the muscular six-foot-four-inch Frush argued, either they paid or did not climb.

Josef Just, a scowling Czechoslovakian with fiery black eyes, a thick black beard, and a chiseled body that would scare a bear expressed the sentiments of the newcomers, growling, "Zis Iss Bullsheeet! You climber, we climber, must share, no pay! Zis Iss Bullsheeet!"

The New Zealand leader, tall and affable Rob Hall, was the diplomat of base camp. He agreed that, perhaps, some compensation should be given. However, since his group and the Czechs planned to climb "alpine style," or in a continuous push without fixed camps, and would thus only be using the ropes a couple of times, they should pay a smaller percentage of the cost. The French arrived splintered into three groups who were barely speaking to each other. One faction was funded by a French insurance company and French Television. Antennae 2 and U.A.P. had already paid nearly forty million francs preparing for a live broadcast from the summit. Their producer, Guy Garibaldi, a man of action not words, decided that it was silly to risk his program for a few thousand dollars and agreed to pay. But he specified that he was not paying for Marc Batard. This set a difficult precedent for the other, less-endowed groups. Rob Hall tried to strike up a deal with Garibaldi whereby French Television could film the Kiwis if they paid their icefall fee. Hall assured him that the film could be sold for a profit in New Zealand. The second French contingent, which sported the festive, phosphorescent glow of pink and yellow "Jean Marc Boivin Extreme Dream" attire was caught in the middle. They agreed, in theory, to pay, but said that they did not have the money with them. The Czechs remained adamant that they would never give in to capitalism on a mountain: "Iss Bullsheeet!"

In the midst of the debate a diminutive Frenchman approached the crowd. "I am Marc!" his voice boomed, like a tiny terrier with the bark of a Great Dane. He had come up from Pheriche that day, normally a three-day trek away. After listening to the problem he announced, "The weather changes, I go tonight." While those negotiating with him were still in mid-sentence, he turned and walked quickly away with his "Marc Batard 24 Hour Everest" support team scurrying after him.

Marc Batard always walks fast. The week before, to acclimatize, the wiry thirty-seven year old speedster from Megeve, France, climbed the world's sixth highest mountain, Cho Oyu, in eighteen hours from base camp. Now he was going to race up Everest, solo and without supplemental oxygen, in under twenty-four hours, broadcasting live on radio back to France. His sponsorship depended on it. He also was rushing to get up before his countrymen, Michel Parmentier and Benoit Chamoux performed a similar feat from the north side. Donning his custom-made, ultralight, bright orange climbing suit with its two-liter bladder for black coffee connected to a straw running up his collar to his mouth and a built-in radio microphone, he signed an I.O.U. without looking at the two pages of legal jargon and, at eight o'clock at night, turned on his headlamp and began dashing up the mountain. Cries of "Allez Marc!" rang out into the darkness until his light bobbed out of sight.

At least the icefall access controversy was settled. The "Extreme Dream" French, the Czechs, and the New Zealanders quickly signed I.O.U.s with varying intentions of paying. Batard stumbled back to camp at six the next evening. He claimed to have reached twenty-six thousand feet before he was stopped by bad snow conditions and exhaustion. Sounding remarkably like Inspector Clousseau, he told me in his heavily accented English, "I don't eat two days, I come Pheriche, I anger and think bad, is no good. Now I eat, then summit maybe."

He rested six days before learning via the radio that Chamoux and Parmentier were making their bid. Batard suited up, poured in the black coffee, and sprinted again, this time leaving at six o'clock in the evening. He passed Camp Two in full stride, at 10:30 P.M., and disappeared up the Lhotse Face. Late the next afternoon I met Marc descending to Camp Three. The skin was drawn tight over his prominent cheekbones. Only his bulging eyes differentiated Batard's thin face from a skull. He seemed to have aged ten years. I gave Marc tea as he muttered, "I make one hundred vertical below top. I can make summit, but I die. I am so sick, every breath vomit, vomit; so I think maybe I go down now or else I die."

Marc was not only dealing with an endurance problem. He was also running his supermarathon with a quarter of the oxygen pressure that exists at sea level. In 1978 Tyrolean climbers Peter Habeler and Reinhold Messner were the first to reach the summit of Everest without supplemental oxygen, a feat physiologists had predicted would be fatal. It was later shown that variances in barometric pressure and in the atmospheric pressure near the equator make it possible, but only barely. Any altitude above eight thousand meters or twenty-six thousand feet is still considered to be in the "death zone" where there is not enough oxygen to sustain life.

Batard's decision was a wise one. We later learned that Michel Parmentier died at twenty-seven thousand feet on his attempt. He became exhausted, collapsed, and Chamoux was unable to bring him down. On the same day a small avalanche hit one of the Spanish tents on the West Ridge killing Narayan Shresta, a high-altitude porter. Shresta was one of the most experienced people on the mountain, having summitted Everest in 1985. Although not a Sherpa, he shared their Buddhist faith, and deserved a proper cremation. It took two days for the Spanish team to lower his body back to base camp. Then, they carried him down to a magnificent hillside under the majestic summits of Taweche and Cholatse. Amidst three dozen *chortens*, or rock memorials, commemorating the lives of Sherpas who died on Everest, Narayan Shresta's soul was released to the wind and a new *chorten* built.

Meanwhile, Chomolungma revealed a gentler side to her personality. The daily monsoon storms stopped. Her flanks basked in the glow of bright sunshine. But, even in perfect weather the lack of oxygen makes movement above twenty-four thousand feet difficult and dangerous. My lungs burned as I climbed the vertical mile of ice to our high camp on the South Col, the saddle between Everest and Lhotse at 26,200 feet. Three or four gasping breaths between steps did little to ease the pain. My mind, dulled by a lack of oxygen, continually urged me to "go ahead, sit down and rest for a while." But I knew that if I stopped I wouldn't go on. I developed a rhythm. Swing the ice axe, take three breaths, move the left foot up and sink the crampon points into the ice, take three breaths, move the right foot up and take four breaths. I continually tricked myself saying, "after fifty steps you can take a rest, Geoff," to be followed by "just kidding, sucker, do fifty more." My mind felt as clear and light as the morning after drinking a fifth of Jack Daniels, six shots of tequila, and a bottle of red wine. I reached the Col at two-thirty in the afternoon. All things considered, I was moving pretty well.

I reflected on the craziness of risking my life for an endeavor so reliant on luck. Five years ago I had been at this altitude ready to try for the top when a storm nearly took my life. Now, I was again within striking distance. Looking down through the cloudless sky on the tiny mountains that had seemed so enormous from below I dared to think I might make it, while silently beseeching Chomolungma to remain kind for a few more days. I thought about my karma and fingered the red string around my neck as I directed my gaze toward the summit ridge.

I traced our route. Above loomed fifteen hundred feet of steep ice leading to the Southeast Ridge. From there we follow the jagged, knife-edged crest to the South Summit, the highest point visible to me. On summit day I would climb solo. There is not enough time to stop and belay and still reach the peak. A rope means two people die instead of one if there is a slip. Regaining my breath on the South Col, I was actually pleased by how strong I felt. I wished that I could continue on up. But we still had to establish our assault camp and stock it with food, fuel, and oxygen before attempting the summit. Securing the ropes in place, I slowly turned to descend.

The weather remained perfect. Every team, except the Spanish who were delayed by the funeral, made rapid progress up the mountain. The first success of the year was claimed by the Czechs. Joseph Just and Duson Becik powered to the 27,890-foot summit of Lhotse via a new route after an all-night push from Camp Three on Everest. They climbed unroped and without supplemental oxygen. A technically difficult first ascent done on the world's fourth highest mountain without supplemental oxygen is a mountaineering coup equivalent to pitching a no hitter and slugging a home run in the ninth inning to win the game 1-0. But, for them, it was merely a training and acclimatization exercise. Along with teammates Peter Bozik and Jaraslov Jasko, they were preparing to attack the most difficult climb ever attempted; an alpine style ascent, without oxygen, of Everest's Southwest Face.

The Czechs were not the only ones with outrageous plans. Jean Marc Boivin lives extreme dreams. The thirty-seven-year-old mountain guide with dancing eyes from Chamonix, France, has been on the forefront of climbing, hang gliding, and extreme skiing for most of his life. Feats like solo climbing the North Face of the Matterhorn, then skiing down its sixty-degree West Face only to climb another route on the North Face and descend by hang glider, all in one day, are routine for him. He came to Everest with his newest toy, a light steerable parachute called a parapente. Boivin was also going to carry skis to the top. Depending on wind and snow conditions he would ski or fly, whichever was more fun.

Marc Batard no longer saw Everest as fun. He wanted to go home. Frozen vocal chords reduced his formerly commanding voice to a barely audible raspy whisper as he lamented, "I must make top, you know. I no want go up more but, is not possible to make sponsors if no success here." So the exhausted man prepared to endure a little discomfort now to insure financial backing for the pleasure of walking to the North Pole, and then the South Pole, in the future.

Meanwhile, my team and the Koreans continued our methodical approach to the mountain. We both prepared high camps and carried up bottled oxygen to support our summit bids. With all of the incredible plans around us, it seemed boring to be just climbing Mount Everest. Johnny "Rotten" Petroske, a deadpan humorist from Seattle who had "Summit or Die" embroidered on his jacket, told the other teams, with a straight face, that he was going to roll down from the summit in a barrel. He calmly explained that his new lightweight barrel had been tested on Niagara Falls and was ready for Everest. I was proud to be introduced as his "pusher." After every explanation of his plans he would thunder, "It is my DESTINY!" In the midst of Marc, the Czechs, and other assorted "extreme dreams" no one batted an eye.

A more controversial issue for my group was the selection of summit teams. Nine of us were strong enough. Frush selected himself, lean and bearded Steve Ruoss, and the small but powerful Stacy Allison for the first try. They retreated back to base camp to rest while the camp at the South Col was being stocked. I felt that we should not have a designated first team down relaxing before our route was fully prepared. We should all work hard until a summit attempt was possible; then those who were strong enough would continue up and those who were not would rest. Unfortunately, Frush held to his decision. We were delayed at least three days by a reduced work staff on the mountain and could not participate in the biggest party Chomolungma has ever had.

At six o'clock in the evening of September 25, Marc left base camp for his third and final charge. Five hours later, the mighty Om left his tent, at twenty-seven thousand feet on the South Pillar, along with another Korean and two Sherpas. At midnight the "extreme dream" team set out from the South Col. Boivin was accompanied by "The Big Swiss," Andre George (who resembles a slimmed-down Andre the Giant), three other French Guides, and three Sherpas. The two groups met at the South Summit, continuing the last hour up the final ridge together. At three-thirty in the afternoon eleven climbers from four different countries embraced on the summit of Mount Everest. An hour later, twenty-two and a half hours after leaving base camp, a "very much exhausted" Marc Batard joined the celebration. His phenomenal speed ascent was soon to be matched by an equally prodigious speed descent.

I was at Camp Two at 21,600 feet when I heard the news from the French radio. Boivin was going to jump. It is true that the day was calm with the jetstream in a rare pause. But seriously, the last idiot to try and use a chute up this high was the crazy Japanese man who found out too late that the air was too thin to slow his ski descent from the South Col. Now, Boivin was going to jump from three thousand feet higher? Taking off from the absolute summit he plummeted like a stone. Then the parapente caught air and he began to soar. He was still just a dot, a mile above me, as he slowly began to lap the cirque of Everest, Lhotse, and Nuptse. Five hundred feet overhead he swung above his canopy. My heart dropped. But he continued on around, completing a perfect flip. He added one more loop for good measure before touching down at Camp Two as lightly as a feather, on his feet, with Everest in the background, the sun at a forty-five degree angle on his face and his hat and glasses off, six feet from his crew of cameramen. The crowd of twenty Sherpas, climbers, and cameramen who witnessed the landing began screaming and applauding. Boivin's youthful face responded with a shy, "What's the big deal?" smile. He had descended eight thousand feet in eleven minutes.

Three days later Stacy, Steve, and Jim left the South Col going for the summit. They expected three Sherpas to come with them, each carrying an extra cylinder of oxygen. Only one, Pasang Gyalzen, arrived. None of them was willing to risk going to the top without extra oxygen. So, Frush decided they should have a lottery. He told Pasang to pick a number between one and ten. Then the three Americans would guess. Whoever was closest would get the gas. Steve picked "six." Stacy said "four." Jim chose "eight." Then they all turned to Pasang.

The slightly built, five-foot-three-inch Sherpa was terrified. He later confided to me, "I think, 'Why they ask me this? Why they make me choose? How to choose?' Then I think, 'Who is nice to give big tip?' I think maybe Stacy give best bonus. So, I say, 'Stacy most close, my number must be three.'" Cursing their bad "luck," Jim and Steve turned back while Stacy climbed into history as the first American woman to reach the summit of Mount Everest. Pasang continued to the top with her, pausing to set the high-altitude cigarette record with a quick smoke on the South Summit. At the peak they met my friend from the ice-fall, Mr. Chung, and two other Koreans for a photo session before descending.

Two days later, on October 1, I returned to the South Col along with Peggy Luce and three Sherpas, Dawa Tsering, Nima Tashi, and Phu Dorje. I had originally been on a third summit team with Johnny Petroske and Don Goodman and was supposed to have been at base camp resting for our attempt. However, I argued that as a doctor I should stay high in case one of the people in the first team had a problem. I knew my body and its reaction to altitude and felt confident that I would be able to go for the top without a rest. Moreover, I was concerned that the spell of good weather would not last, and thought that it was likely that a spot would open on an earlier attempt. Sure enough, both Diana Dailey and Jean Ellis from the designated second team became ill and turned back from Camp Three. I was at Camp Two. Jim Frush called on the radio and asked if I could go up and join Peggy and the three Sherpas. I left immediately. By staying high I made my own luck. I ascended the Lhotse Face to the South Col knowing that this was my shot at the top of the world.

We spent the afternoon melting snow into water and listening to the wind shake the tent. The wind intensified during the night. Down valley clouds began to build for the first time in a week. I remembered watching a similar change in the weather in 1983. At midnight, when we planned to leave, it was impossible to stand outside the tents. At one o'clock it was no better. We finally left at two, leaning into the eighty-mile-per-hour gusts. Carrying an eighteen-pound oxygen tank, an extra pair of mittens, a little water, and no bivouac gear, I was committed to making the top and descending back to camp.

Climbing by moonlight, we made good progress up the icy slopes. "One slip and you are dead, concentrate!" I kept commanding myself. Focusing on my breathing, I tried to ignore the rapid pounding in my chest. At the South Summit I met the Korean leader, Mr. Nam, who had timed his ascent to coincide with the closing ceremony of the Seoul Olympiad. Bracing ourselves against the wind, we continued up the steep and narrow ridge leading to the peak of the world. Above the forty-foot rock obstacle known as the Hillary Step, unadulterated joy welled up inside of me. I knew that I was going to reach the summit of Mount Everest. The peak seemed to be just ahead. But when I reached the ridge crest, another, higher point rose above me. Chomolungma teased me with several more false summits before the ridge dropped sharply away. The world spread out beneath me. I spent fifteen minutes savoring life as the highest person on earth, alone on the six-foot-by-three-foot platform of ice that is the top of the world.

The summit of Mount Everest was everything I had fantasized it to be and more. Mr. Nam, Dawa Tsering Sherpa, Nima Tashi Sherpa, Phu Dorje Sherpa, and Peggy Luce also made it. I placed a pink plastic lawn flamingo on top and tied an American flag around its neck. I also left pictures of my family and a girlfriend and chopped out some stones. After forty-five minutes at the summit, I renewed my concentration and started down. I contemplated taking Boivin's skis and boots which were stashed in the snow glowing with their "extreme dream" logo. I decided that it was not worth the increased chance of a fall and continued descending as fast as I could. Like Boivin I returned to Camp Two before dark. I did not learn until later that Peggy fell on the descent. By luck she arrested inches from an eight-thousand-foot plunge. She lost her sunglasses and quickly became snowblind. Fortunately, Dawa Tsering stayed behind and guided her down safely. They spent the night at the South Col and returned to Camp Two, in deteriorating weather, the next day.

Chomolungma had now allowed a record twenty-three of us on her crest, but a two-day storm signaled that her mood had changed. Back at base camp I celebrated success with Om and Duson Becik. Having no language in common mattered little. Our communication was perfect. We gesticulated about life and made plans to climb together next year. Duson showed pictures of his two children and we teased Om about sheep. We exchanged summit stones from Lhotse and Everest and drank Slivovich until we all passed out.

Not everyone was celebrating. Three groups had not been able to capitalize on the good weather. The Spanish failed on the West Ridge. French Television could not begin their live broadcasts until October 4 because their satellite was being used for the Olympics. And the New Zealanders could not find a route to climb. The Kiwis shared a permit with the Czechs but were not willing to try either the route on Lhotse or the Southwest Face of Everest because of the difficulty and danger. Rob Hall tried, without success, to get his four-person team permission for the Korean route.

Lydia Brady, a smiling, sleek, twenty-five-year-old free spirit with long blond dreadlocks from Christ Church, New Zealand, was not happy with the situation. Lydia was one of the most experienced female mountaineers in the world. Her sights were firmly fixed on Everest. She was already banned from climbing in Pakistan for scaling twenty-six-thousand-foot Gasherbrum 2 without a permit. Dancing by herself on the glacier, with heavy metal blasting from her boom box, she told me she was going to be the first woman to climb Everest without oxygen even if she had to go solo and on the sly. Lydia also lays claim to the unofficial high-altitude sex record. When confronted with the possibility that her achievement may have been surpassed in 1987, she retorted, "But we both had orgasms, mate." If she got there with a willing and capable partner Lydia hoped to set an unbeatable high-altitude sex record on top of Everest. She had it all planned out, with a summit suit that featured resealable Velcro and rip-stop nylon flaps in her windsuit that provided easy access to a series of slits in her inner layers of clothing that became perfectly aligned when she bent over.

When the skies cleared, a large plume of snow was blowing off of Everest from the North indicating that the jetstream had lowered. Undaunted, several teams continued the assault. My teammates Don Goodman, Johnny Petroske, Dave Hambly, and Diana Daily, as well as Ruoss and Frush still had summit aspirations. The French Television was now broadcasting live and needed to reach the top with their camera. To increase the odds they invited four of the strongest Spanish and two Sherpas to join them. Lydia and two other Kiwis prepared to climb while Hall continued to negotiate for an easier route. Meanwhile, Joseph Just readied himself for the Southwest Face. As his final detail he asked, "You have drug for all or nussing?" After obtaining eight tablets of dextroamphetamine, he headed up the mountain with Duson, Jaraslov Jasko, and Peter Bozik. Bozik had recently made the first ascent of the "magic line" on K2, the world's second highest mountain. That climb, also done without supplemental oxygen, was the hardest big mountain route yet done. But, he said, "Ziss iss most more diffeecult!"

The crowd gathered at Camp Two to wait for a break in the wind. Every day saw the annihilation of two or three tents. Travel between tents was often impossible. Radio communication to base camp was difficult to understand over the howling wind. Its roar was slightly less on October 12. Five Chamonix guides acting as cameramen, four Spaniards, and five Sherpas rushed to the South Col. Most of the tents had been blown apart, and they spent a sleepless night crammed seven to a tent. The next day the wind picked up again. French Cameraman Serge Koenig persevered with Sherpas Pasang Temba and Lhakpa Sonam. Everyone else retreated back to the Col.

Koenig and Lhakpa Sonam made the top. The cable connecting the camera to the transmitter broke and there was no live broadcast. I was in the French Television control tent. The director was on the radio swearing at Koenig, demanding that he fix it. Koenig replied in a cracking voice, "Impossible!" adding that he was cold and exhausted and must come down. Amid further swearing the commentator sent the excited message of "Serge Koenig au Sommet!" along with views from base camp back to France. The director walked in circles declaring, "C'est une tragedie!"

Chomolungma quickly reminded everyone what is really tragic. Neither Sherpa returned to the South Col. A frostbitten Koenig surmised that they had fallen descending behind him. Then, as if to mock the efforts of the day, the winds suddenly abated. At midnight the four Spanish and two Sherpas prepared to leave for a summit try. Leaving the tent they encountered a blond woman with dreadlocks. "D'ya mind if I tag along, mate?" Lydia asked.

She had started early the previous evening from Camp Three. The Spanish shrugged and headed up. Lydia stopped to melt snow for a drink, falling far behind. An hour from camp the Spanish came upon what, at first, looked like a large rock in the snow. It was the twisted and frozen body of Pasang Temba. A little higher they found his brother's body. They continued up to the South Summit where Sergei Martinez became very weak. Giving Martinez all of their remaining oxygen to use while waiting, Jeronimo Lopez, Nil Bohigas, Luis Giver, Nima Rita, and Ang Rita pushed on to the top. It was Ang Rita Sherpa's record fifth time to the summit of Mount Everest without supplemental oxygen.

Meanwhile, in an effort to take advantage of the lull in the wind, Steve Ruoss and Johnny Petroske headed for the South Col. The four Czechs also prepared to leave. The first ascent of the Southwest Face required six camps, 180 bottles of oxygen, 160 Sherpas, thirty-five climbers, six thousand feet of fixed rope and over a month of climbing. The Czechs brought two sleeping bags for four people, two days' worth of food, and a small stove with fuel to melt snow for three days. Even if they completed the ascent in three days, they would be climbing without supplemental oxygen in the "death zone," above twenty-six thousand feet, where there is barely enough oxygen to sustain life, longer than anyone had ever survived at that height.

Steve and Johnny's climb did not last very long. Halfway up the Lhotse ice face a body went hurtling past them. They immediately turned back to see if the climber was alive and needed help. When they reached the body they found it was the now-mutilated remains of Lhakpa Sonam Sherpa. The French had thrown the two dead bodies down the mile-high ice cliff without telling any of the other teams via the radio. The other body hung up on rocks and never made it down.

The Spanish summit team returned to find Sergei lapsing in and out of consciousness. They used rope to make a basket to drag and lower him in. Leaving the South Summit they met

Lydia crawling upward on all fours. It was already 4:30 P.M. They told her to descend. She refused. Already overextended and fearing that Sergei would die, they did not argue. Ang Rita looked her in the eye and said, "You are going to die!" before she crawled out of sight.

Down at base camp Lydia's teammates were informed by the French radio that she was making her solo bid to be the first woman up Everest without oxygen. They discussed the situation and decided to leave for Katmandu. Rob Hall explained that she was told that they did not have a permit and that he was concerned that her illegal ascent would result in a climbing ban on other New Zealand climbers. So, he was off to the capital to negotiate with the Nepalese Ministry of Tourism, not knowing if his teammate was alive or dead.

The exhausted Spaniards dragged Sergei back to camp at 8:30 P.M. My team gave permission to use our oxygen. When they went to get the mask they found Lydia crawling around outside the tent. She said she made the summit, but couldn't find her tent. They pointed her in the right direction and watched her crawl away. Even with the oxygen, Sergei was worse in the morning. At his best he was blind and unable to walk. They began lowering him down the Lhotse face. Steve and Johnny tried to go up again. But when they saw the condition of the Spanish, they turned around to help. It took twelve hours to retreat as far as Camp Three. Ruoss, a physician, examined Sergei and decided that he had severe cerebral edema and almost no chance for survival. The next day Sergei was lowered to Camp Two where Ruoss gave intravenous medicines and put him in an experimental "Gamow Bag" that increases atmospheric pressure to simulate a descent of six thousand feet. Finally, twenty climbers, representing every team, carried him down through the Khumbu Icefall to base camp. The French Television helicopter then evacuated Sergei, along with Luis Giver, who had severe frostbite, to Katmandu. Both were safe in a hospital in Spain two days later.

Although temporarily lost during the confusion, Lydia reappeared at base camp, walking upright, but still having to face the

Nepalese authorities. In order to lessen her fine, Lydia told authorities in Katmandu that she had climbed on the mountain without a proper permit, but that she did not make the summit. This cast considerable doubt on her later claims to be the first woman to climb Mount Everest without supplemental oxygen. Personally, I am absolutely certain that she made it. I write this based on knowing Lydia as a person, having spoken to her immediately upon her descent, and because the conditions on the mountain were such that it was much more difficult and dangerous to descend from the South Summit than to continue over the Hillary Step, where there was a fixed rope, and on up to the top. If Lydia really were so exhausted that she could not make the peak, she would have died on the descent.

As the drama of the Spanish and Lydia resolved, a more intense one started. The Czechs called on the radio to say that they completed their ascent of the Southwest Face reaching the South Summit at 8:30 P.M. on October 17. Having taken one day longer than expected, they were out of food and fuel. This night at twenty-nine thousand feet was their third above twenty-six thousand feet without oxygen or a tent. They said that they were tired and dehydrated but otherwise fine. They planned to summit the next morning and descend via the South Col. On October 18 Joseph Just pushed on to the top alone.

He joined his companions on the descent. In their last radio transmission, at four o'clock, they said that three of the four were blind and all were exhausted, but they were on their way down to the South Col. At base camp I paced back and forth thinking about Duson fighting for his life up above, but there was nothing that I could do. Don Goodman, Diana Daily, and Dave Hambly went to the South Col. No one was visible. The next morning the jetstream winds returned with a vengeance. No further trace of the Czechs was found.

In all, an amazing thirty-one people reached the summit of Mount Everest during the post-monsoon season of 1988. Nine died trying. Leaving the mountain in the wake of tragedy it was hard to find meaning in my accomplishment. On the other side of the planet Bobby McFerrin was rising to the top of the popular music charts preaching, "don't worry, be happy." The Sherpas have a similar philosophy, "Kay Guarnay." Literally, this translates into, "What to do when there is nothing to do?" Practically, they don't worry about what they can't control, and are very happy. Here I was, and there was nothing more that I could do. Touching the red string around my neck, I repeated "Kay Guarnay" and began the long walk back to Katmandu.

Following the Heart

"YOU ARE SUCH A ROMANTIC MAN. Surely, I must save all my love for you!" This was the message waiting for me when I returned from Everest, thanks to satellite communication and French Television. On my way in to the mountain I had met, and became infatuated with, a woman. She was beautiful, with shining dark hair and sparkling blue eyes. Athletic and funny, she had a fantastically quick mind that was readily apparent despite our not knowing each other's language. I sat next to her in a small cafe in the Thamel district of Katmandu. She said her name was Ariane and that she had just graduated from the conservatory in Lyon, France, where she had trained as a classical pianist. That afternoon we rode bicycles out through the lush paddy fields along the ring road that surrounds the city. For the next two days we explored together, visiting Hindu and Buddhist holy places and walking hand in hand through the narrow streets of the city. On the last evening before I started trekking into Mount Everest, I suggested that we spend the night together. Ariane said, "No! I do not even know you three days. I cannot sleep with you!" With that, she kissed me on both cheeks and vanished into the night.

Two months later I returned to base camp, having just reached the top of the world. French Television was broadcasting live back to France from base camp every day. They asked to interview me. At the conclusion of our discussion about climbing to the summit I asked if I could say hello to my friend, Ariane, a pianist in Lyon. The announcer became very excited and began babbling in French, "Blah blah blah blah, AMOUR! Blah

blah blah blah blah AMERICAN blah blah blah SUMMIT blah blah blah blah AMOUR!" He then turned to me and said, "I have say that you make the summit of the world for the love of your French girlfriend, Ariane, and that you dedicate the climbing of Mount Everest to her. This is true, no?!"

A few months later I met up with Ariane again and we spent enough time together to get to know each other and share some wonderful moments. Ultimately, however, her life was music, and mine led elsewhere.

After Everest I followed my heart and became a full-time professional climber. My medical career would have to wait for awhile. I have found that it is best to flow with life's opportunities rather than fight the current attempting to follow a preconceived plan. I worked as a mountain guide, finding great joy in sharing my love of the high places. I found a niche creating international custom dream trips that included technical climbs. These adventures brought me to all seven continents and allowed me to get to know many interesting people, and to climb many of my fantasy mountains and routes. Between paid trips, I continued attempting routes that stretched my limits. These were now a level below the hardest climbs that were being done on a world scale. I have come to appreciate that my climbs and my dreams need only be significant to myself. I never set out to "conquer" a mountain, which to me sounds as ridiculous as trying to "conquer" a woman. The great French climber, Lionel Terray, described mountaineers as, "Conquistadors of the Useless." As in any meaningful love relationship the only purpose served by climbing a mountain is the happiness and enlightenment gained by the person who does it; if you approach it looking only toward what you can expect to "get," you will most likely come away with nothing.

Antarctic Solitude

"ANOTHER STEAK, GEOFFREY?" my host asks, refilling my cup with fresh coffee. My stomach is already expanded from polishing off sixteen ounces of fine Argentine filet and a baked potato. However, the taste of the salsa is still dancing on my tongue.

"Gracias," I reply, stretching my bare feet near the gas heater. Colonel Campos, the host, nods to Juanco, the burly mechanic at the stove. Juanco peels a ripe avocado into the hot sauce and in one motion spears a sizzling steak from the grill and fries an egg to put on top. The aroma is magnificent. All in all, the rescue seems to be progressing well.

Then, into the cozy Weatherhaven hut stomp three snow-encrusted figures, icicles drooping from their mustaches and beards. Mugs Stump is the first to speak. "We couldn't get to them. The ridge is too steep for the snowmobiles. We'll have to carry him down."

"Steak?" I mumble while chewing. I hand my plate to Paul and reach for my parka, windsuit, and overboots.

"No thanks, mate. I'm still stuffed from the lobster tails I had at brekkie," Paul replies.

Four thousand vertical feet above us, in a tiny tent pitched in the center of a topless igloo, Peter waits. His right forefoot is black, swollen, and puffed with fluid-filled blisters the size of golf balls. Severe frostbite causes intense pain. All of our narcotics are in my medical kit at base camp. With Peter are the rest of my team: Klaus, a professional mountaineer from Munich who is Peter's partner; Ken, the novice from New York who is now so exhausted he can barely walk; and Rob, the mountain guide from Canada who climbed the wrong mountain. Three hours ago I spoke to them on our walkie talkie. I happily reported that I had made it over the Col, then climbed down the ice face and through the whiteout ground blizzard to the Chilean Air Force Camp. I explained how my private radio transmission was intercepted and expanded into a full-blown crisis by the bored radio operators at bases throughout the continent before I finally reached the National Science Foundation geology expedition who are stranded twenty kilometers away. They had cheerfully agreed to disregard their orders and evacuate Peter and Ken with their snowmobiles. My partners are expecting help any moment. But we are again learning that down here nothing comes as expected. As Hugh Culver, the managing partner of Adventure Network, is fond of saying, "Hey, this is Antarctica."

On March 5, 1908 six members of Shackleton's Nimrod Expedition left Cape Royds man-hauling a three-meter sledge laden with 1,230 pounds of supplies. Their goal was to ascend twelve-thousand-foot Mount Erebus. Five days later they proved it possible to climb a mountain on the Antarctic continent. Douglass Mawson uncorked a bottle of champagne when the climbing party returned to the boat, but chloroform was also required for the amputation of Sir Philip Brocklehurst's frostbitten big toe.

The highest mountain in Antarctica is 16,863-foot Mount Vinson in the Sentinel Range. Located seventy-eight degrees south, its summit is arguably the coldest and most remote place on earth. Mount Vinson was first contacted by a living animal in 1967 when the ten-man American Antarctic Mountaineering Expedition, led by Nick Clinch and supported by U.S. military planes, succeeded in making the first ascents of the three highest peaks on the continent. The next people to visit the Sentinel Range came in 1983. Dick Bass and Frank Well's "Seven Summits" expedition hired Giles Kershaw, the world's most experienced polar pilot, and a modified Tri Turbo airplane to make the second ascent of Mount Vinson. Kershaw returned a year later to climb the mountain with Canadian mountaineer Pat Morrow, and the pair began contemplating a commercial airline for adventurers in Antarctica.

Punta Arenas, Chile, is a port town at the Southern tip of Patagonia. It is the last stop for ships passing from the Atlantic to the Pacific and home of Mary Teresa's, the world's oldest continuously active brothel. Punta Arenas is also the base for Adventure Network's Antarctic Airways. They specialize in flying support for all manner of adventures in Antarctica. This year they are supplying a multinational crossing of the continent with dogsleds led by Will Steger and Jean-Louis Etienne and simultaneously a crossing of Antarctica on skis by Reinhold Messner and Arved Fuchs. They are also running tourist flights to the South Pole, and will fly me to the base of Mount Vinson. Being both a doctor and mountain guide, I was hired by Adventure Network to come to Vinson and lead their four commercial clients to its summit.

I wondered who would pay over twenty thousand dollars to vacation at the world's coldest and most remote big mountain. The only one of my clients I'd heard of before the trip was Ken Kammler, a forty-six-year-old surgeon from New York. Soft-spoken and hard of hearing from a diving accident that damaged both eardrums, Ken has the quiet confidence of a man who has succeeded in many endeavors. Unfortunately, climbing mountains isn't one of them. He had taken introductory rock and ice climbing courses in New Hampshire, but had never attempted a big mountain or been winter camping. As for the remaining expedition members, all I knew was that one resided in Germany, one in Canada, and one in the Netherlands.

In December 1989 I rendezvous with my other climbing partners at the Cabo Des Hornos Hotel, a six-story red Georgian building abutting Punta Arenas' town square and dominating the skyline from the harbor. Peter Kinchen is a white-haired and bearded Dutch business man who looks like Santa Claus after completing a Charles Atlas course, and he wants to climb Mount Vinson, badly. In the last two years he has scaled Mount

McKinley and twenty-three-thousand-foot Aconcagua in Argentina. Still, he knows the limitations of being fifty-two years old. To acclimatize for Antarctica he spent the previous ten days in the mountains of Ecuador. As a final assurance, he paid full fare for his own personal guide, Klaus Wagner, to join us. Wagner is a German mountain guide who has taken Peter to the top of many mountains. Dark-set and serious, he is focused on the task at hand. "It is a big mountain and I am sure very cold. To guide these people to the top will not be easy," he cautioned in perfect, but heavily accented English.

But, the trip may be easier than I expected. The final "client" is Rob Mitchell, a mountain guide and naturalist from Calgary, Canada. An upscale Canadian adventure travel company sent Rob to investigate Antarctica; they are thinking of offering a Vinson climb in 1991 and want their guide to be familiar with the mountain. Wiry and energetic with a mischievous grin, Rob is a professional adventurer. He has his own travel company whose custom offerings have included everything from the Paris-Dakar road rally to climbing in the Ruwenzori Mountains. He talks softly but gives the impression of always having something important to say. When Rob speaks, we listen. Lighting a cigarette, he tells us, "I leave every environment a bit better than I find it." Our group vows not only to leave no garbage in Antarctica, where any refuse is preserved forever, but to clean up any trash we encounter while there.

"Americano, Dance?" a smiling teenage girl in a blue satin negligee shyly asks, her perfumed hand grazing my shoulder. The pulsating beat of Latin music fills the room, a silver reflecting ball sends patterns of light across the darkened hardwood floor onto Chilean business executives, Japanese sailors, and an international assortment of scientists and adventurers dancing with the girls of the house. Three days after arriving in Chile I am standing at the bar of Mary Teresa's, straining to hear what Hugh Culver says. "The big problem is the fuel," he says. "The start of the season was delayed by bad weather. We couldn't get our fuel flights in. And we lost a fuel drop that we paid the Chilean Air Force to make."

The bottom line is that we are delayed at least another week. A full flight of fuel has to go in before any people can go. Ordering another bottle of fine Chilean Cabernet Savingon, Culver talks of the difficulties Adventure Network is having keeping the twelve-million-dollar transantarctic dogsled expedition supplied and how Reinhold Messner and Arved Fuchs' attempt to ski across the continent was delayed so long they were forced to abandon their goal of traversing the ice and now are just crossing the continental land mass. Adventure Network is flying logistical support for both big-budget trips as well as having organized my trip. With a wry smile Culver keeps repeating one phrase like a mantra, "Hey, this is Antarctica!"

At the outskirts of town Rob Mitchell, naturalist, points out the dorsal fin of an Orca cutting the azure waters of the Straits of Magellan. "Watch now, there'll be another one. Orcas always travel in pairs. This time of year they come up on the beach to take seal cubs. They'll grab a few cubs and bring 'em out to deep water to share. Killer whales are playful. They toss 'em around a bit before eating them," he lectures.

An hour later we arrive at a penguin rookery. "These are Magellanic penguins," Rob tells us. "Penguins don't have any natural predators on land, but several animals and birds will go for their eggs. The Magellanics dig nesting holes to protect the eggs." He shows us how to approach large groups, downwind, without disturbing them and leads us to a nesting hole where a mother penguin watches a solitary egg. Carefully distracting the mother, Rob gently removes the egg to point out salient features. Then, with a slow hand, he replaces the egg in the nest. The mother whirls and sharply pecks her beak deep into the egg. Yellow-white ooze drips from her perplexed face and seeps from the myriad of cracks in the egg. Rob Mitchell, naturalist, suggests we head for Patagonia.

The Towers of Paine rise abruptly for a vertical half mile from the Patagonian plain. At the base of the spectacular gray and black formation is a clear blue reflecting pond punctuated by gnarled icebergs that break away from the glacier at the base of the peaks. At the far end of the lake the water drops off to a cascade of white water. On an island in the center of the lake, accessible by a long footbridge, is the Hosteria Pehoe, serving fresh fish and Chilean wines that do justice to the views. The hiking is phenomenal, with plenty of guanacos and giant rheas to keep Rob talking. But, the longer we stay in Patagonia the more I see the life of our climb in Antarctica seeping away like a cracked egg. Klaus has to guide in India in a month, Ken has surgery scheduled, and Peter is worried about spending so much time away from his new wife. When we call the Adventure Network office they tell us to stay a few more days. Only Rob Mitchell seems to be having fun.

With time to kill back in Punta Arenas, dinners become prolonged affairs with fresh king crab, giant mussels the size of biceps, and thick Argentine steaks served by sloe-eyed waiters who reinforce the fact that we are in a land where mañana doesn't mean "tomorrow," but simply "not today." Also awaiting a flight to Antarctica are French and American film teams that are supposed to record the transantarctic dogsled expedition reaching the South Pole, two Saudi Arabian scientists who hope to be the first Arabs at the Pole, and "Cricket," a mathematician from Chamonix who is the logistical coordinator for Will Steger and Jean-Louis Etienne's trip across the continent. Radio reports update the dogsledders' progress three times per day. They are already past the last resupply point before reaching the Pole. Meanwhile the press covering Reinhold Messner is in a near panic as he has not been heard from in nearly two weeks. Then, Giles Kershaw arrives and things start to happen.

Despite being a founding partner of Adventure Network, Kershaw works most of the year flying jumbo jets out of Hong Kong for Cathay Pacific Airlines. It is now his vacation. He will fly a single-engine Cessna 185 across the Drake Passage and then buzz around Antarctica on holiday with fellow pilot Max Wenden. Mild mannered and youthful appearing, despite a few gray hairs in his neatly trimmed beard, Kershaw was the driving force behind the British Antarctic Survey and was also the hero of several well-publicized Arctic and Antarctic rescues. His diplomatic skills and clipped British Public School accent ease everyone's tension. As if on cue, Messner radios in to say he is fine and had just turned his radio off. Then the good news continues as it is announced that our flight is set to go.

Looking at the ancient DC 6 brings the cracked egg back to mind. Duct tape is ubiquitous. A couple of dozen temporary seats are fastened along one side. The majority of cargo space is taken up by fuel drums. We load our gear onto the plane and move our vigil to the airport. The stories we hear from the journalists do not help my confidence. The previous ABC crew had been similarly delayed along with Messner and Fuchs. The first time the group got airborne they turned back from sixty-nine degrees south because of headwinds. The next attempt reached the Antarctic Peninsula before a generator and engine caught fire, forcing them to limp back to Punta Arenas with three propellers. During that flight Messner turned to Rick Ridgeway, who was covering the Steger expedition for ABC, and said, "Rick, I have survived more fucking things than you can imagine, and now I am going to die on this airplane, I know it," before turning to stare out at the swirling seas of the Drake Passage. On the next attempt the plane broke down on its way to the gas pump. The passengers were sent back to the bar for a "short delay." Ridgeway looked out the window, saw the engine in pieces on the tarmac and decided to go home. The rest of the group finally made it to the Patriot Hills camp, Adventure Network's base camp in Antarctica which consists of a half dozen Weatherhaven shelters. Then the journalists were stranded at Patriot Hills awaiting a flight out for seventeen days, renaming Patriot Hills, "The White Coffin," as they watched their supplies dwindle.

Back in the bar at "Aeropuerto PPTE Carlos," Giles tries to reassure everyone, saying, "I've inspected the engines myself. The plane is in excellent repair. As soon as the weather clears, you're off." I am more soothed by Peter Henning, a dangerous-assignment specialist for ABC and a former fighter pilot. He was buying drinks at the bar. Finally, the weather report clears and we put on full Antarctic clothing and climb the aluminum painter's ladder into the unheated, nonpressurized cargo plane to settle into the canvas frame seats. With us are a couple of reluctant replacement sled dogs, the two Saudis whose religion prevents drinking alcoholic beverages and who seem more nervous than everyone but the dogs, the French and American film crews, and "Cricket," the field coordinator for the dogsled expedition, who assists with everything. At two-thirty in the afternoon, Rick, a laid-back, long-haired flight engineer locks the hatch, points out the can in the back, and wishes us a good flight. Upon takeoff, cameraman Gordon Wiltsie pulls out his sleeping bag and pad, spreads them on the floor, and goes to sleep. Peter Henning and the French film crew keep the party going for the entire eight-hour flight.

Out the window the white wilderness stretches to the horizon. Endless white, punctuated by giant crevasses and a few rock mountains, extends on and on. After eight hours of flying over glimmering white desert, the plane lowers and banks steeply to land on the blue ice runway at the base of the Patriot Hills Mountains. It is eleven o'clock at night. We step out into bright sunshine and a sharp, cold wind. Snowmobiles drag sleds with our gear while we walk thirty minutes across the ice to Adventure Network's base in Antarctica. Five semi-permanent Weatherhaven tents are secured to the ice. Eight sled dogs eye us from a chain adjacent to the camp. Inside the cook tent a gas heater continually melts iceblocks into water, and the smell of steaming fresh chicken soup with homemade black bread greets our arrival. Peter cracks a new bottle, dons a Penguin hat, and the party continues into the night.

It is good company, but having come this far we are anxious to reach the solitude of Mount Vinson. We are informed we will be stuck at the "White Coffin" for "several days." The Steger group is three days from the South Pole, and Adventure Network's Twin Otter will be busy shuttling the journalists and Saudis to the pole to meet them. Then Messner and Fuchs are desperate for a resupply, so they are the next priority. After that, "weather permitting," we can fly.

Klaus is shaking mad. "I must be in India by the end of the month!" he shouts. "This is not possible. We cannot wait," he berates me as we use a woodcutter's saw to cut blocks of ice to build a windbreak to protect our tents.

At six in the morning we lie down to sleep. But, with the bright sunlight and tension, I barely close my eyes. I am just starting to doze when I hear the hum of an engine.

I crawl out of my sleeping bag and peer from the tent to see a tiny orange single-engine aircraft circling above camp before landing gently on skis a few hundred feet from our tent. Giles Kershaw and fellow pilot Max Wendon have smiles as bright as the sun reflecting on the snow. They made the first single-engine crossing of the Drake passage by putting a fuel drum on the back seat and using a homemade pump apparatus leading to the fuel tanks. For the past twenty-four hours they alternated pumping fuel and flying. Giles steps from the plane, hatless and gloveless, wearing a leather flier's jacket and tennis shoes amidst down coats, oversized mittens, and mukluks. He strolls over and says, "I'll just have a nap, then I'll fly you over to Vinson. Can you be packed in, say, three hours?"

In three flights of one and a half hours each, Giles and Max take us over the most spectacular rib of mountains I have ever seen. The Sentinel Range is of Himalayan grandeur. Although Vinson tops out at 16,864 feet, the mountains rise eight thousand feet from the Antarctic plateau with no foothills. Behind them, a seemingly infinite sea of whiteness extends forever. We set down, smoothly, in a snowy valley under the massive, vertical, West Buttress of Mount Tyree. Mount Shinn and Mount Epperly also rise impressively in the foreground, blocking our view of Mount Vinson.

Before they leave, Max and Giles help us build an igloo of snow blocks around our base camp tents, and then we all settle in for a long sleep. With the constant high sun the days blend into one. We adopt a schedule of working and climbing for roughly twenty hours followed by ten to twelve hours of rest. One sleep later, we melt a couple of pots of snow on our MSR stoves, give Giles and Max a final brew of warm tea, and watch the orange Cessna rise from the snow, wave its wing, and leave us to climb our mountain. We have a radio which is set to a frequency that Patriot Hills will begin monitoring in eight days. Until then, we have a mountain to climb.

The first task is to secure our base camp against the Antarctic winds and to create an area in which to cook and melt ice to drink. The two weeks of delays in Chile bonded us as a team. We spend a long day preparing camp. It is difficult work as our bodies must adjust to the eight-thousand-foot altitude and minus twenty-five degree temperatures.

While sawing the ice into building blocks we hit buried refuse from previous expeditions. The cracked penguin egg comes back to mind as a metaphor for man in Antarctica. The world's fifth largest continent is dotted with twenty-five major research stations. Three thousand tourists visit its coast every year on cruise ships, and adventurers such as ourselves and the trans-Antarctic teams are starting to invade the interior. Although none plan to cause any harm, litter from an American scientific survey in 1967 is preserved in the ice as fresh as the garbage left by climbers a year ago. Two-thirds of the world's fresh water is preserved in the ice of Antarctica. Despite the chill and the well-publicized ozone hole, the air here is the freshest on Earth. Gazing down the crest of the range and out onto the Antarctic plateau where no traces of life are visible to the horizon, I can only think of how lucky I am to be here, now.

After another sleep we set out to make an acclimatization ascent of a small peak west of base camp. The climb is straightforward, and a few hours later we arrive on top. Back at Mary Teresa's, a girl had asked Rob, "Who is the most popular singer in North America?"

He instantly replied, "Sonny Bono!" Klaus and the girl both expressed surprise. They hadn't heard of him. Ken and I assured them that Sonny Bono is the greatest entertainer in history. We decide to name the hill "Point Sonny Bono." We are about to join hands and sing "I Got You Babe," when we look down and see two planes and a cluster of tents on the other side of the mountain.

Thirty minutes later, we arrive at a Chilean Air Force camp. Colonel Campos is in charge. He welcomes us with lots of orange juice, hot coffee, and fresh apples. He tells us that a month ago a Chilean plane had a hard landing here, damaging its nose. Another plane flew in with mechanics, welders, and engineers to repair the damaged aircraft. He estimates that they will be around for another ten days. "We have plenty of food and fuel. Come back anytime," he says before we leave for the short walk back to our camp.

One sleep later we carry heavy packs to the site of our first camp on the mountain, at the base of a steep ice face. It is just a long walk, but once we top a knoll, the Chileans are far below. We think we are finally alone with our climb. After building a snow wall, we cache our loads and return to base. We crawl into our base camp igloo complex and sleep for twelve hours, then bring the rest of the gear up to Camp One. Ken, Peter, and Rob complete the igloo around the tents while Klaus and I fix a rope on the ice wall. We cook a good pasta dinner and melt lots of ice to drink. Just as I finish the ritual of stripping off four layers of clothing and wiggling into my tight, overstuffed, down and Gore-Tex sleeping bag, I hear a strange roar approach and suddenly die.

"Howdy, mate," a Kiwi accent greets me. Outside the igloo are three snowmobiles with "Harley Davidson" motorcycle decals on them. Sitting astride a vehicle marked "Humpy From Hell" is Paul Fitzgerald, a geologist from New Zealand. Fitzgerald is gathering rock samples for an American National Science Foundation project to determine the mineral composition and age of the Sentinel Mountains. With him are two mountain guides, Rob Hall and Mugs Stump. "We're camped twenty kilometers away," Paul says. "We saw your plane land and thought we should pay a call."

"Would you like some tea?" I ask.

"Naw, not necessary," Paul replies. "We've got a big heater going, melting snow, over at our camp. We're done with our work, and are just cruising about, waiting to get picked up. We've waited a week already. It doesn't look like the NSF is coming anytime soon. When you get off your climb, call us on radio frequency 4445 and we'll party. We've got lobster tails, steaks, and Mexican food," Paul says with a smile.

Above Camp One our route of ascent goes over the fifteen-hundred-foot ice wall where Klaus and I secure the fixed rope. We carry heavy loads up the steep slope, self-belaying with mechanical ascenders. Ken has not done this kind of climbing before. At ten thousand feet we review basic technique. Klaus climbs with Peter. I stay with Ken, who struggles to keep his balance, alternating between desperate pulls with his arms and hesitant, scratching steps with his crampon points sliding on the ice. We lag far behind Klaus, and Peter. Climbing alone, Rob Mitchell, mountain guide, reaches the col at the top of the face by the time Ken and I cross the bergschrund at the bottom. Seven tense hours later I look down on a fairy tale valley leading to the massive bulk of Mount Vinson. Sweat drips from Ken's forehead. He collapses from exhaustion on top, resting thirty minutes before regaining his feet for the gentle descent to camp.

We descend five hundred feet to a snowfield where Peter, Klaus and Rob have almost finished building another protective wall. Rob Mitchell, gourmet, flashes his impish grin and yells, "booty!" while holding up a can of king crab and a jar of black caviar that he excavated from the refuse of a previous expedition. He hands Ken some water.

Despite his dehydration, Ken takes only a small sip before passing the water to me. Then, smiling, Ken grabs a saw and asks, "What should I do?"

In unison Rob and I answer, "Take off your wet clothes!" I am shocked to see that every layer is soaking wet.

Fortunately the sky is a deep cloudless blue, and Camp Two basks in twenty-four hours of direct sunshine. There is a steady breeze and no humidity. Ken strips and crawls into his down sleeping bag. Rob and I hang the drenched clothes on ski poles. In seconds they freeze solid. Shaking off the ice quickly yields a dry ensemble, but Ken's flagging physical condition and lack of climbing experience are bigger problems.

Mount Vinson towers four thousand vertical feet above us. To gain the peak we must surmount three thousand feet of steep

Rock Climbing
in the Shawangunks
(photo John Sherman).

Bob Shapiro returns
to the scene of his
ancestors' work.

On the summit of Point
John, Diamond Buttress
and ice-window on Mt.
Kenya in background
(photo Bob Shapiro).

Mt. Kilimanjaro.

M'Buti Pygmy, Okabal,
enjoying *bangee* in the
Ituri Forest.

With M'Buti Pygmies,
of the Ituri Forest
in Zaire.

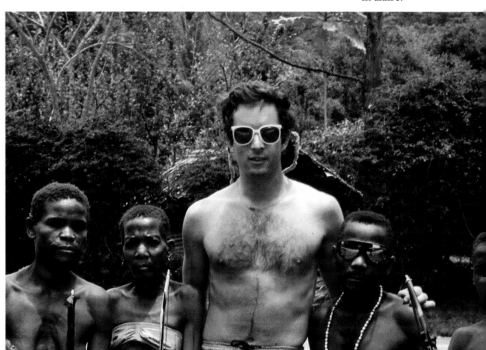

Leroy Kelm and team
at his landing strip,
Jayapura, Irian Jaya
about to fly us to
Carstensz Pyramid.

Dani tribesman,
Wanimbo, using organic
needle and thread in
Irian Jaya, New Guinea.

Dani men enjoying a
meal of bat.

Seppanus always wanted
to be a writer, too.

Sam Moses on the
North Face of
Carstensz Pyramid.

Native snow wear,
Kebowaks on the
Summit of Carstensz
Pyramid (L–R Bob, Sam,
Geoff).

Carl Tobin, the Mountain Biker from Hell *(photo Roman Dial)*.

Ken Kammler on the Summit of Mt. Vinson, Antarctica.

Summit of Mt. Kosciusko, Australia with John Fantini—gaining the strength of a monkey, or are we just glad to see each other?

(photo Mike Hayes)

The Matterhorn, North Face—My only early climbing goal was to scale the three great North Faces of the Alps, the Matterhorn, Eiger and Grandes Jorasses *(photo Phil Lieberman)*.

On the Summit of Aconcagua, South America.

With Scott Woolems at the Apex of North America, Denali.

The Potala Palace,
Lhasa, Tibet.

Meeting Sir Edmund
Hillary on the approach
to the East Face of Mt.
Everest, 1981.

(photo Jim Morrissey)

The East Face of Mt. Everest.

The Kangshung Team, 1983 (1st row L–R: Dan Reid, Lou Reichardt, Me, Jim Morrissey, George Lowe, Dave Cheesmond; 2nd row: Carlos Buhler, Andy Harvard, Kim Momb, Jay Cassell, Carl Tobin, Dave Coombs, Chris Kopczynski).

The Bowling Alley—
East Face of Mt. Everest.

Dave Coombs climbing on
the East Face of Mt. Everest
(photo George Lowe).

The rock headwall on the East Face of Mt. Everest *(photo Jay Cassell)*.

Dan Reid, 1983.

Pujah ceremony, base
camp of Mt. Everest,
1988.

Lydia Bradey.

In the Khumbu ice-fall,
Everest 1988.

Avalanche in the
Khumbu ice-fall.

J.M. Boivin descending from the summit of Mt. Everest, 8,000 feet in 9 minutes.

The first plastic lawn flamingo on top of Mt. Everest. Stacy Allison, the first American woman, and Pasang Gyalzen Sherpa (*photo Stacy Allison Collection*).

Me on top of the world, Mt. Everest, October 2, 1988 (*photo Dawa Tsering Sherpa*).

snow ridge to reach the plateau between Vinson and Mount Shinn. Then, a long, flat, crevassed section has to be traversed before we reach the summit cone. I anticipate our summit day will take fifteen hours, which does not bode well for Ken. Seven hours, at lower altitude, nearly pushed him into a coma.

We defrost the cans of caviar and crab in boiling water and enjoy a pleasant soiree despite wine steward Rob Mitchell's inability to produce Dom Perignon. Klaus says, "It is best for Peter to take a long rest, drink, and then climb to the top. With this much cold, at this altitude, waiting will make him weaker. I think we should go to the summit from this camp. Messner told me it is best. There is too much wind on the saddle."

Peter smiles and says, "Ja, this is best." Ken is sound asleep, barely waking long enough to gulp the cups of hot soup we bring him.

Another sleep later Rob, Klaus, and I fire up all three stoves to melt snow and begin hydrating. Ken still looks tired, but claims he is ready to go. Peter is determined to leave as soon as possible. I believe Ken would benefit from a rest day, but I also want to keep the team together.

The final factor in the decision to push for the summit is the weather, which seems to be changing. For the first time, high cumulus clouds lace the sky. After discussing the options among the group we decide to leave as a team. But if Ken and I move too slowly on the first snow ridge, the two of us will turn back. We drink as much as possible, fill our thermos bottles (insulated water bottles freeze solid in minutes) and tie into the rope. I am again climbing with Ken. Klaus is taking Peter. Rob Mitchell, mountain guide, starts out breaking trail, climbing solo.

Short-roped with Ken, I reach the col between Vinson and Shinn after five hours. We rest to nibble chocolate, sip warm tea, and put on an additional layer of clothing. A strong wind gusts along the plateau. The mercury in Peter's thermometer retreats beneath the forty-below mark to the bottom of the bulb. Ahead are five distinct summits and it is difficult to tell which is the highest. Distances are deceiving. We plod ahead for two hours and seem no closer. But as the sun moves behind the peak and we enter shadow, it seems colder. I am wearing two pairs of heavyweight polypropylene underwear, bib overalls, a jacket made of thick pile, a one-piece insulated windproof suit, goggles, a neoprene facemask, three layers on the head and hands, vapor-barrier socks, plastic boots with alveolite inners, and neoprene overboots. And I am still cold.

"How're ya doing, Ken?" I yell into the wind from two feet away. He just stares straight ahead. I try again. Nothing. Finally, I realize that his hearing aids have frozen. He can't hear me shouting next to him. Grabbing him, I get the message across. Ken gives a thumbs up sign. Climbing on, our team spreads apart. Rob moves faster, vanishing from sight above us, Klaus and Peter slowly drop behind despite the fact that Ken and I are moving at a pace of one step per four raw breaths. Reaching the base of the final impressive summit pyramid we pause and look around. The sky is still blue with a few high cumulus clouds. Below, two figures are slowly descending into a swirling mist of windblown snow. Another is climbing steadily upward

Five hundred vertical feet beneath the top Klaus joins us. "Peter is so tired, he must go down. Rob exhausted himself climbing the wrong peak and is helping Peter down. I make tracks for you and wait on the summit," he screams into the wind. Klaus moves smoothly and confidently, unroped, up the forty-five-degree ice. Ken and I slow down. Ten breaths per step. Ten steps then a sitting rest for Ken. When I motion that we must go down, Ken shakes his head. We have been climbing for sixteen hours. If we were anywhere else I'd insist on turning back. Here, the weather is still perfect and we don't have to worry about darkness. If we can't make it now, Ken won't be able to make another bid on this trip. It has cost him a lot of time and money to get this close. He shows no signs of altitude sickness and assures me that he is warm. So, we continue, inching for the continental climax.

Above the steep ice we rest and finish our water. There is only a short, easy final ridge to the top. Klaus passes us on the way down. "It is the greatest summit I have made, with the best view. It's better than Himalayas or anywhere," Klaus joyously exclaims. I point to Ken and ask Klaus to please wait and help me bring him down. "I cannot. My feet are so cold. I do not feel my heel. I waited on top for you but it was too cold. I must go down," he insists and begins downclimbing the ice. Ken gathers his incredible inner fortitude and pushes onward and upward. An hour later we embrace on the pinnacle of Mount Vinson. Klaus was right on two counts: The views are incredible, looking down on the jagged summits of the Sentinel Mountains and out over the vast white wilderness. And it is cold.

The descent takes nine careful hours. When we reach the bottom of the ridge, with only a flat walk to the tents, Ken can only manage five steps in a row before sinking to the snow to rest. A quarter mile from camp Klaus meets us with a liter of raspberry drink. Again Ken has only a small sip before handing me the juice. Returning to camp we get warm congratulatory hugs from Rob, who is tending the stove.

Rob Mitchell, solo explorer, confirms that he climbed the wrong summit. He cheerfully tells us, "I was a long way up before I realized it wasn't the highest. But, it was a good climb and probably a first ascent. I'll go back up after we sleep. Anyway, Peter needed me to take him down. He was very tired. I'm worried about his right foot. It was frozen solid when we got down."

Klaus adds, "I kept asking him if he was warm enough, every thirty minutes. He always says, 'Ja, fine.'"

Peter snores loudly from his tent. I shake him awake, yelling, "Peter, how is your foot?"

"Good," he mumbles, then he slides his head down in to his bag and resumes snoring.

There is nothing more I can do now. Ken and I drink a few cups of water and quickly join Peter in slumber. Round trip, our summit "day" took twenty-seven hours of continuous climbing.

Eighteen hours of sleep later, I am the first awake. While fumbling to prime the first stove I hear Peter groan. Walking to the tent door I see him staring at his right foot which is peeking out the side of his unzipped sleeping bag.

"My foot is bad, Ja?" he asks.

I look. The first three toes are black, the entire foot is swollen to twice normal size and huge blisters have already formed. "How did this happen, Peter?" I ask, rhetorically, while beginning to think about what to do. It is a serious situation. Peter won't be able to put on his boot or weight the foot. If the blisters break and the foot gets infected he might die. First, we have to get him down.

"It didn't hurt yesterday," Peter mentions flatly, looking in wonder at the deformity at the end of his leg.

"It must have been frozen solid and numb," I explain, to no one in particular, as the full gravity of the situation starts to hit me.

Titus Oates developed severe frostbite on his right foot while returning from the South Pole in 1912. He spoke to his commander, Robert Falcon Scott, saying that he did not want to be a burden to the team. Scott's diary entry from March 16 records that the temperature was minus forty degrees. Oates's famous last words, spoken before leaving the tent to vanish in a raging blizzard, were, "I am just going outside and may be some time."

Klaus, Rob, and I discuss the options. It looks possible to bring a snowmobile around from the next valley to reach us. This will be the least traumatic way to transport Peter. We agree that I should go over the hill behind us and down the steep ice to the Chilean Air Force camp where I can radio the geologists for help.

When I top the crest I see a thick layer of clouds rolling in beneath me, stretching as far as I can see. Descending the fixed rope I am enveloped in mist, and it suddenly grows very cold. Visibility is less than three feet. Luckily, I can follow our trail in the snow through the whiteout. If I lose the track, I will die. I retrace the route, hoping I've picked the right path to the Chilean camp. Just as my worry starts to escalate into panic, I stumble out of the mist into a warm welcome at the Chilean camp.

"Ola!" Colonel Campos says. "Have some juice. Here, I make you steak. Do you want rice or potato?"

The Chilean radio operator is unable to reach the NSF geological party. However, our message is intercepted by the operator at the American Amundsen—Scott station at the South Pole, who monitors their field team's radio frequency twenty-four hours a day.

"Tell me what you want with them," the operator demands.

"It is for rescue of climber," the Chilean radio operator answers in broken English.

I take the microphone to say, "It's nothing serious. Only a little frostbite that will be a little safer to move by snowmobile." But it is too late. The chain of protocol has started.

"I have to check with the head of operations to see if this is within policy," comes the NSF woman's curt reply. In the next hour, increasingly exaggerated reports of the "dying" climber are the talk of Antarctica. South Pole calls Siple. Siple station calls Rothera base. Rothera contacts Marsh. Marsh radios Punta Arenas. In a giant game of telephone, word of Peter's near-fatal condition spreads. Everyone is contacted except the people we want. The Adventure Network team at Patriot Hills calls the Chilean camp to say they will send a plane carrying a snowmobile for us as soon as the weather improves. Meanwhile, there is nothing I can do but drink Chilean coffee with milk and cookies.

Three hours later Mugs, Rob, and Paul roar up to the Chilean camp. "What's goin' on?" Mugs asks. "The American bases are goin' ape crazy over this. You shouldn't of told those jerks a thing. It takes fifty of 'em a week to decide if they can take a shit. They can't get their act together to get us out, yet they try and tell us what we can or can't do. They said not to do anything until some commander reviews the situation. You're climbers. So are we. Fuck them. What do you need?"

I explain the situation to Mugs.

"No problem! Be back with your boys in a few hours," Mugs says optimistically. The rescue squad fires up their engines and sets off into the mist.

I tell my team the plan via walkie-talkie. Peter and Ken will come out by snowmobile with some of the gear. Klaus and Rob will climb down bringing the rest of our stuff. I wanted to go up with the snowmobiles, but we decided that an additional person would not be needed and might prevent one vehicle from negotiating the steep incline up to camp. There is nothing I can do but settle in for my third major meal in as many hours.

Feeling terrible about Peter's frostbite, I mull over my decisions to this point. Perhaps we should have established a higher camp? Perhaps I should have stayed with Peter and sent Rob to get help? Or maybe we should have just carried Peter down, keeping the team together? As a doctor I want to minimize the chance of infection and don't want to risk popping the blisters by lowering him down the fixed ropes. Then again, I don't want him to stay at high altitude. Perhaps I shouldn't have taken Ken to the summit when I saw two of my teammates descending. All the major decisions were made after extensive discussion with Klaus and Rob, both professional mountain guides. However, I am the trip leader, and ultimately responsible for the outcome. On a big mountain you have to choose what you think is the best option at the time and go with it. Luckily, I've reached the geologists. They will bring Peter down quickly, without traumatizing his foot.

But, no! The snowmobiles can't reach our camp. "The ridge is too steep," Mugs smiles, then quickly adds, "Let's go up and carry him down."

Rob Hall, Mugs, and I climb back up the ice face with Mugs dragging a sled behind him to the top. Meanwhile, Klaus and Rob Mitchell carry Peter to the crest. Ken staggers up on his own. We carefully place Peter in the sled and pad him well. Rob Hall, Klaus, and Mugs lower Peter down the fixed ropes. I belay Ken. Rob Mitchell, sanitation engineer, heads back to Camp Two to clear our camp and carry out all the garbage left by previous expeditions. At the bottom of the face Paul and the snowmobiles wait to take us to camp. Later we'll use the snowmobiles to carry the trash from the mountain.

The rescue is successful, but an Antarctic storm blows in and it is five days before the weather improves. Peter remains optimistic and cheerful, staying in the hospitable warmth of the

Chilean camp. Ken and I start him on antibiotics and painkillers and change his dressings twice each day. When my supply of Vaseline gauze gets low, I replenish it from a medical kit left by the first ascent expedition in 1967. We shuttle between camps by snowmobile and dine like kings. Finally, the weather clears enough to try and evacuate us. Unfortunately, the fog closes in again while the rescue plane is in the air. The Twin Otter is forced to land fifteen kilometers away, which is close enough, as our snowmobile taxi service takes us, our gear, and the garbage to the plane. Mugs is so fed up with the NSF being unable to get him out, he asks to leave with us. Adventure Network says "yes," but the "Commandant" tells him no. Since his passport is with the NSF and he hasn't been paid, he stays on the ground.

Back at the "White Coffin" we again join journalists, Saudis, and sled dogs waiting for a flight. The situation sounds bad.

"One engine is broken. We've sent to Miami for a new one," is the radio message from Punta Arenas. Moreover, they need a mechanic who knows how to install a DC 6 engine. Klaus is going to miss his trip, Ken will have to revise his surgery schedule, and we are all terrified that Peter's foot will become infected. The blisters have popped and we are running out of dressings again. We finish my supply of antibiotics but, fortunately, there are extra antibiotics intended for the sled dogs at Patriot Hills.

The British Imperial Trans-Antarctic Expedition of 1915 appeared doomed. Their ship, Endurance, was crushed by ice in a grinding tragedy of twisted wood. Twenty-eight men faced food and fuel shortages, the threat of killer whales, and the inevitable crack up of the ice floes beneath them. Sir Ernest Shackelton and five others repaired a twenty-foot boat and embarked on an eight-hundred-mile voyage across the savage seas of the Drake Passage. After sixteen days at sea the men reached South Georgia Island where they had to cross glaciers and a previously unpassed mountain range to find help for their mates trapped in Antarctica.

If it weren't for my concern over Peter's foot getting infected, our wait would be tolerable. Gordon Wiltsie and I climb the Patriot Hills with telemark skis and enjoy some great runs. John

Stetson, the trainer for Will Steger's dogs, explains mushing. The cook tent steams with fresh simmering soups and is often the scene of lively international debates. But the camp's mood slowly turns ugly. The journalists aren't going to make it home for Christmas. Everyone else thinks he will lose his job, wife, or girlfriend. Klaus begins insisting that Ken and I declare Peter's condition to be terminal, so we can get an emergency military evacuation.

Finally, the radio announces that the DC 6 is fixed. But we are then told the pilot has quit. Only ten hours later, the cavalry arrives in the form of a big DC 6 filling the sky above camp. Giles Kershaw is again sitting tall in the saddle. He has "nipped back from Hong Kong" to rescue us from the ice. We reach Punta Arenas at six the following morning. Klaus and Ken fly to Santiago at seven, still wearing their mountain clothes. Giles arranges for a Chilean Air Force jet to evacuate Peter, who will have three toes amputated back in Europe. Returning to town, I find that all of my clothes have been stolen. Rob Mitchell, haberdasher, insists that I take his extra pants, socks, and shirts.

As the sun sets on us for the first time in weeks we head out, clad in sandals, slacks and short-sleeved shirts, to celebrate our return to Punta Arenas. A spectacular double rainbow appears in the sky, revealing all of the colors hidden in white light. Rob Mitchell, poet, happily exclaims, "Hey, this isn't Antarctica!"

Seven Summits: Adventures on Seven Continents

I NEVER SET OUT SPECIFICALLY TO CLIMB to the highest point on all seven continents, but having climbed Mount Vinson, I was past all of the most difficult obstacles to joining the seven summits club: the small group of people who have stood on the highest point of all seven continents. I have never been goal oriented in my climbing, focusing more on the present and enjoying the process of my climbs, and I have turned back short of the top many more times than I reached the summit on mountains. Many of my best climbs and adventures have taken place on small, little-known peaks and rock outcrops. With the exception of Mount Everest, I have never thought about climbing a mountain just because it was the biggest. In both my romantic life and climbs, I look for quality. I have never wanted to make love to a woman just because she was the largest one around.

Nonetheless, my moments have brought me to the peaks of Carstensz Pyramid (16,023 feet, in Australasia) Mount Kilimanjaro (19,340 feet, in Africa), Mount McKinley, or Denali (20,320 feet, in North America), Cerro Aconcagua (22,873 feet, in South America), Mount Elbrus (18,481 feet, in Europe), Mount Vinson (16,864 feet, in Antarctica), and of course, Asia's Mount Everest (29,028 feet). But, when I think of the "Seven Summits," I think of the great adventures I have had on each continent and the people who shared them with me.

My trip to Carstensz Pyramid was, in retrospect, my favorite adventure. It had uncertainty at every step, was the best climb of the continental summits from both a technical and from the pure fun-o-meter standpoint; and the journey was my greatest cross-cultural experience. Some have argued that the highest point for the continent must be on Australia proper, which is a small dirt dome called Mount Kosciusko (7,316 feet). I find this argument to be silly. It is like saying Japan is not in Asia. I have walked up Kosciusko. When I think of Australian climbing, I don't think of hiking up little hills. My mind drifts to an incredible quantity of quality rock in perfect sunshine, and bananas. I had a high-speed tour of Aussie rock with a wonderful eccentric who has probably done more first ascents of rock climbs than anyone in history, John Fantini. Fantini is a fanatic with an insatiable drive to climb virgin rock. He credits his climbing longevity and energy to his "modified fruititarian" diet. On hard climbing days he eats only bananas, believing that they "give you the strength of a monkey, Mate." Before I was fully aware of his culinary ideas, I agreed to go with John into Bungonia Gorge to do the "longest, hardest free rock climb in Oz," called "Siblings of the Sun." John gave me all of the climbing equipment to carry on the hike in to the route, while he shouldered a larger pack than mine, saying he was bringing the food. From the size of his load, I thought we would be dining in style. I imagined a two-burner stove, gourmet recipes, and plenty of Cooper's Lager. Instead, I was shocked to see that all he brought to eat were two bushels of bananas. When I questioned his choice, he looked me in the eye and said, "Geoff, this is a 'ard climb! You'll need the bananas, Mate!" It was, and I did.

Beyond climbing, I found adventure "Down Under" diving among sharks on the Great Barrier Reef and descending into a canyon with a madman. Nic Bendeli, a sometime teacher and full-time fun hog, met us in Sydney when we groggily emerged from a seventeen-hour flight. Nic's five A.M. grin beamed with adrenaline. "Welcome, Mates. Ready for a little canyoning?"

We drove through early morning mist, winding up from Sydney Harbor on cobblestone streets to wake up one of his "Mates" and borrow an extra wetsuit. "You'll love it!" Nic assured us. "It's got everything: climbing, swimming, exploration, beauty, and adventure."

"It's bloody cold and people die," his Mate added less enthusi-astically before going back to bed.

We then headed for the Blue Mountains, a two-hour drive away. The first stop was Katoomba for a "typical Aussie brekkie" of fruit salad (fresh Kiwi, passion fruit, berries, pineapple, and three kinds of melon), eggs, grilled sirloin steak, potatoes, homemade bread, cappuccino with fresh cream, and rice pud-ding with cinnamon. "Righto," Nic said, grinning while he pol-ished off the last bite. "Let's go have some fun!"

The next stop was "Clostral Canyon." We parked the car on top of a peak in a range of rolling mountains covered with dense eucalyptus forest giving a blue-green tone to the landscape. Nic doled out our gear: full wetsuits including hoods, one rope each, climbing harnesses, and descending devices. The manic grin returned, as Nic shouldered his pack and loped down a narrow muddy trail into what seemed to be just a wide valley. After a few minutes we picked up a spring that led to a small stream that cut a narrow trough into the limestone hill. The canyon was barely five feet wide. Trees overgrew the top. We descended into an ever-darkening hidden chasm, alternately jumping from stone to stone and clinging to the walls in a desperate effort to keep dry.

Then, as if to mock our efforts, we came to "Devil's Chim-ney," where the canyon becomes a river with the walls over-hanging five hundred feet on either side. My friend Mike Hayes and I had come to the land of Oz to rock climb in the sunshine and scuba dive in the balmy waters of the Great Barrier Reef. We now found ourselves shivering on top of a large chalkstone wedged fifteen feet above black, icy rapids. We put on our wet-suits and surveyed the landscape. Once we took the plunge there would be no turning back, no way out, but through.

"Righto!" Nic yelled as he jumped into the current. Mike and I saw him bobbing away, sucked in our breath, and followed. The water was barely above freezing, crystal clear and drinkable. For the next four hours we swam, rappelled, and scrambled down the canyon. The walls grew progressively higher with ferns and moss clinging to the sides giving an amazing range of green shades when sunlight pierced down into the chasm. Three times we fought the current to set up rappels. We then slid down our ropes, through waterfalls, to continue. Finally, we reached a sandbank at the merge of Rainbow Canyon. Nic pulled a dry bag from his pack and brought out crackers, fruit, Brie, Camembert, smoked oysters, and a flask of white wine. "Good on ya, Mates!" he exclaimed. One more hour of slightly easier scrambling and swimming led to our exit point and a two-hour hike out. Walking up the trail I looked at where we had been. Completely overgrown by trees at the top, the twenty-five-hundred-foot-deep chasm was invisible. The sun glowed orange near the horizon as we dragged ourselves back to the car. Kookaburras serenaded us from the treetops and kangaroos boinged alongside the highway as we drove back to town.

I still have not made it to Bob Shapiro's rock spires in the Sahara. But, I have had some of my best adventures in Africa. Mount Kenya, of course, was a peak that changed my climbing focus and remains a favorite. I also climbed on some of Kenya's numerous crags with the local master, Ian Allen. We scaled beautiful, clean rock in the Rift Valley, while magnificent birds of prey circled overhead and zebras and giraffes grazed down below. From an animal-watching perspective my favorite trip was going to the Virunga Volcanoes of Zaire to observe the mountain gorillas. It was a joy to sit in close proximity to our fantastic wild relatives. From the volcanoes, I went to the wildest natural environment I have seen anywhere on the planet, the Ruwenzori Mountains on the border of Uganda and Zaire.

The Ruwenzori are Ptolemy's mythical "Mountains of the Moon," the postulated source of the Nile. I approached the range from Zaire in 1990. The approach trek began in thick rain forest. The path rose through a primeval bog of giant ferns. Next, I moved up into a magical realm of overgrown heather trees rising forty feet and dripping to the ground with Spanish moss, where I tread on a thick carpet of bright green moss that collapsed like foam rubber under foot. Above this layer was an ecological zone of bizarre foliage. Fifty-foot groundsels and lobelias led up, past sparkling pure lakes, to the spectacular glaciated peaks. I made one memorable ascent, climbing solo up a route of mixed rock, ice, and snow directly up the West Face of Mount Stanley, to the apex of the range, Point Margahrita.

The third glaciated area in Africa is the fabled "Snows of Kilimanjaro." Kili shimmers, like a mirage, visible for hundreds of miles on the high East African plateau. I first gazed upon the peak from the Masai Amboseli game reserve in Kenya in 1979. Unfortunately, the border was closed between Kenya and Tanzania. It was a decade before I surveyed the world from the top of Africa. I walked, with my friend Pam Douglas, up the standard route to the summit of Mount Kilimanjaro. It is a pleasant hike that follows a well-worn path, past three beautiful camping areas with huts built by Norwegian aid workers. It was sad for me to see the number of tourists suffering from altitude sickness on Kilimanjaro. The Tanzanian government charges a large daily fee to be in "Kilimanjaro National Park" and locals tell people the ascent takes five days. Most parties rush up the mountain without acclimatizing properly, trying to save money or because they think it is the thing to do. The result is that few make the top and those that do usually feel awful. Pam and I took an extra day to adjust to the height, exploring Mawenzi, the lower rock summit of Kilimanjaro. This extra day of acclimatization allowed us both to feel great on the peak. Summit day starts from Kibo Hut and wanders up loose volcanic scree to reach the edge of the crater at Gilman's Point. A short walk around the rim with dramatic views, both down into the crater and out across Africa, takes us to Uhuru Point, at the top of Africa.

After the Kilimanjaro climb I attempted to return to Nairobi. At the border between Kenya and Tanzania an elderly Masai woman approached me. She wore traditional robes of red cloth. Brightly colored beaded plates hung from her neck and dangled from her elongated earlobes. Her braided hair was coated with ocher. Two feet from my face she began to sing a song and dance in a flowing motion that sent her neck plates bobbing through the air. When I failed to respond with a cash donation she snatched my festive yellow "Solar" sunglasses from my head as payment for the unrequested show. The sight of her in primitive dress and high tech glasses cracked me up. I snapped a quick photograph. Now I'd done it. She demanded payment for the picture. I tried to get my sunglasses back, but she believed they were now rightfully hers for the dance.

Moments later I was in a Tanzanian police station, under arrest. A burly man in a Khaki uniform two sizes too small told me, "It is forbidden to photograph Masai without payment!" Twenty minutes later I had bribed one policeman for my camera and another for my film. My sunglasses were long gone. At least I saw a "traditional" dance for less than most tourists.

Western influence and the quest for the almighty dollar are destroying the great cultures of Africa as rapidly and terribly as poachers' bullets are killing the rhino. Few places are safe from both the political turmoil endemic in Africa and the devastating invasion of tourists. One of the last bastions of untouched Africa is the Ituri in Northeastern Zaire. Only one road pierces the vast tropical rain forest that is home to approximately thirty thousand Mbuti Pygmies, among the world's most ancient peoples and one of the last groups of hunter-gatherers.

I travelled North from Beni hoping to meet the gentle nomads of the jungle. I knew from Colin Turnbull's classic book *The Forest People* that the Pygmies had a centuries-old symbiotic relationship with the Bantu tribesmen who live along the trans-African road. The Pygmies traded fresh game, honey, and herbal medicines for cloth, metal tips for their arrows, and cookware. With no plan in mind I followed the heavily rutted dirt road, into the Ituri.

In front of a thatched Bantu home near Mount Hoyo, I noticed a freshly killed antelope. I inquired. Indeed it had been traded by a Pygmy that morning. I was told that a group was camped near the Loya River. I hired a Bantu with a dugout canoe to bring me upriver to the Pygmy camp. We stopped at a game trail leading from the shore. Less than five minutes' walk into the thick foliage brought me to a clearing with half a dozen low, green bun-shaped leaf huts. In the shadows were small, shy people. I sat and played a slow blues on my harmonica. They slowly came forward. Men wearing loincloths, bare-breasted women, and naked children surrounded me. The tallest adult stood only four and a half feet. Warm smiles greeted me, we touched hands, gesticulated, and slowly got comfortable with each other.

The next day we left at dawn for a hunting and gathering expedition into the jungle. We followed game paths overgrown with vines. The tiny, barefoot pygmies cruised easily while, with my clumsy large body, I had to alternately crawl on my belly or climb through branches. I struggled to keep up. The thick rain forest was like a shopping mall for my Pygmy companions. They saw things that were invisible to my untrained eyes and heard things that my ears did not understand. The lead hunter, Okabal, spotted a beehive high in a tree. In seconds a burning ember was produced wrapped in a banana leaf. It was covered with damp wood and fanned into flame. Others had gathered ferns that produced a thick, foul-smelling smoke. The smoke bomb was wrapped. Okabal carried it over his shoulder as he climbed seventy feet up the tree to reach the hive. The bees were smoked out, everyone had a nice honey meal and we moved on. The whole process took fifteen minutes.

I could not help but think back to Turnbull's description of when he took one of his Pygmy friends out of the jungle for the first time. They went to the Serengeti Plain. For the first time the man of the forest saw a great herd of wild animals. Turnbull expected his companion to get excited and want to go hunting, as he usually had to work hard to find game. Instead, the Pygmy began to laugh hysterically. Turnbull asked what was so funny. The man answered that all the animals were small like insects. Having never been in the open before, he did not understand how the perception of size changes at a distance.

Similarly, being unaccustomed to the dense foliage, I was not able to see beyond the trees, while the Pygmies saw the full richness of their forest environment. My companions shot monkeys with poison-tipped arrows. Duikers and other antelope were flushed from the darkness by women and children pounding the forest floor with ferns wrapped tightly in vines. The terrified animals ran into woven nets that the warriors stretched across the game trails. Herbs, roots and fruits were gathered as we searched for game. "Bangi," a wild forest marijuana plant was picked and wrapped in vines.

My companions shared everything equally, showing no signs of jealousy. They laughed easily. By the time we returned to the temporary settlement near the river I was aware that Western society could learn much from the Pygmies. I wondered how the inevitable interaction with the outside world would affect the Mbuti.

A few days later, Okabal passed me a long plantain stem pipe filled with Bangi. Taking a drag of smooth pungent smoke, I looked down at my companion. His white teeth glimmered in a single ray of light piercing the forest canopy. Placing my hand on his shoulder I sighed, "You are a cool mother fucker!"

Staring up at me with gentle eyes Okabal repeated, "Coo muhuh fuh."

Perhaps it was his quizzical expression or the way he focused on my mouth, but something made me slowly say the words again. "Cool mother fucker."

"Coo Muhuh Fuhuh," he parroted with a satisfied grin, while four other warriors, Arwhy, Tukutay, Sepee, and Ashunun, crowded around us.

"No." I enunciated each syllable carefully, "Cool Mother Fucker!"

"Cool Muthuh Fuckuh!" said Okabal.

"Coo Muhuh Fuhuh," repeated a chorus of six Pygmy voices. I started laughing. Everyone else laughed at me laughing.

In moments every male in the village was laughing, clapping, and chanting, "COOL MOTHER FUCKER! COOL MOTH-ER FUCKER!" A couple of drums were produced. The assembly stood and danced to the beat.

There are still plenty of adventure opportunities left in North America. A frequent climbing destination for me has been the desert Southwest. Two spires on the Navajo Indian Reservation stand out as favorites. My ascent with Tom Dickey of the "Totem Pole," a six-hundred-foot sandstone needle in Arizona and climbing the massive New Mexican landmark "Shiprock" with Carl Tobin, both had a spiritual quality for me based on their beauty, history, tradition, and the partner with whom I shared the experience.

Rob Slater, Charlie Fowler, Tom Dickey, and I have a tradition of climbing together in the Southwest every winter. Our expedition tee shirts started out with a joke tourist picture of Castelton Tower. The next year we headed for Mexican Hat Rock with the logo, "It's not a Tower it's a Hat." The Totem Pole inspired the, "It's not a Hat it's a Pole," slogan. The next year Tom Dickey and I went on an "It's not a Pole, it's a Hose," ice climbing trip to Telluride, Colorado, with our goal being the "Ames Ice Hose," a difficult frozen waterfall.

Tom and I were dropped at the road head, where the hike to the climb begins, early in the morning. We told our ride that we expected to be out by three in the afternoon. If we weren't at the road, we told him, it meant that we finished earlier and had hitchhiked back to town. The approach was a struggle, wading through hip-deep snow. The climb had very thin ice coating the rock for the first few hundred feet. If we swung our axes too hard they would bounce off the rock. Too soft a swing did not penetrate the brittle ice. Our crampon points had to balance on tiny, precarious, icy rock nubbins. It was impossible to protect the climbing with anchors, so that a fall would have serious consequences. The climb took us longer than we had expected. We reached the top of the climb at dark and had difficulty finding our way down. Next came the slog back out to the mining access road, which was, by that time, deserted. We trudged the six miles back to Telluride. We had run out of water early in the day and were very thirsty.

The first building Tom and I approached as we came into town was the convention center. We entered hoping to find a water fountain and encountered the "Telluride Wine Festival." A matronly lady at the registration desk demanded to know who we were. Surveying the guest list I saw the names of people who had not yet checked in. I pointed at her sheet and said, "Here we are. We are the Goldstein Brothers, Wine Merchants of Colorado Springs." Without batting an eye, she gave us our official name tags and entrance badges for the Australian wine tasting that was in progress. Clad in smelly, wet pile, we entered the hall and joined a formally attired convention of wine experts. They sniffed, swished, spat, and then cleansed their palates before the next taste. Tom and I shot the wine down as fast as it was handed to us. We were soon sloshed. A bit later a woman confronted us. She wanted to know who we really were and what we did for a living as we "obviously aren't wine merchants!" Tom, who was then working a few months of the year as a commercial fisherman in Alaska and climbing the rest of the year, glared at her with wild eyes bulging from his bearded face and roared, "I kill fish! With my bare hands! As many as I can! Then I sell their flesh for money!" No one else disturbed our celebration of the Hose.

Mountain bikes add a new dimension to back country travel. Fat tires, light weight, and eighteen gears make it possible to follow virtually any trail. Carl Tobin, my buddy from Everest, is now a top-ranked mountain bike racer. He has been pushing off-road riding to its limit. With a couple of friends he has pioneered the concept of "Hell biking." Dramatic, lightweight, commando bicycle crossings of three different Alaskan mountain ranges have sealed his reputation as "The Mountain Biker from Hell," going where there are no trails.

George Lowe, Jay Cassell, Carl, and I were teammates on the Kangshung Face expedition in 1983. We decided to have a reunion mountain bike trip. Having never been on a multi-day or off-trail ride, I suggested a luxury outing supported by a chase vehicle carrying camping equipment and plenty of good food and water. Carl was incredulous at the idea of support, or even going where support could reach us, saying, "Leave everything to me, just show up in Hanksville, Utah, at midnight!"

I asked Carl how many miles he planned for us to ride in a day. "Don't think in terms of miles. It's time. We'll ride all the daylight hours, and most of the nights." When I started to discuss food, Carl cut me off. "We'll bring just enough calories to survive," he said, adding, "We're going to ride, not eat!" Next came the question of equipment. "Leave your tent and sleeping bag at home, we're going to ride, not camp!" Next came the issue of water. I wasn't reassured by Carl's response. "Water could be a serious problem!"

For our five-day trip we each wore a small day pack and had a medium-sized stuffsack bungeed to the back of the bike. Our gear consisted of one pair of shorts, socks and shoes, a single polypropylene top and bottom, and a windjacket each. "We are going to ride, not change clothes!" For survival we had a bivouac sack and four liters of water bottles per man. Team gear included a small first aid kit, bike repair tools, two extra innertubes, water purification tablets, matches, and ten pounds of food.

The uncrossable rapids of the Green River divide Canyonlands National Park. The eastern side is easily accessible from Moab, Utah, and crowded with bikers, hikers, and four-wheel-drive vehicles. We would explore the wild western half which has the same great terrain and views as the east, but virtually no people. Carl's plan was to follow Poison Spring Canyon to the Dirty Devil River, portage across, and follow North Hatch Canyon until it dead ends at the base of a large mesa labeled "Big Ridge" on our topographical map. We would climb the mesa, carrying our bikes, then search for water. Red circles on our map marked the "springs" and "seeps."

The ride started out on a firm dirt road and we made good time to the Dirty Devil. After refilling our water bottles with the muddy gray sludge of the river we had a cool bath and then struggled to ride up the dry creek bed of North Hatch Canyon. Every few minutes we hit sand that forced everyone except Carl to walk and push the bikes. We then veered up a side canyon and were soon carrying our bikes up steep scree. A glance at the map proved we were lost. Carl smiled. "Most of my best adventures start when I'm off route," he said, as he started carrying his bike down a cliff where a fall meant certain death.

After sixteen hours of strenuous riding and portaging our bikes we looked up at a twenty-five-hundred-foot climb to gain the "Big Ridge." The situation was serious. We were out of water and the desert heat had taken its toll on our bodies. The topographical map showed a "Seep," four miles from the top of the mesa. Carl and George were stronger and climbed ahead with the plan that they would find the water. Jay and I struggled to gain the top of the mesa by moonlight. We found a flat area to sleep and build a big fire. My tongue was swollen and completely filled my dry mouth. After an eternity, Carl and George returned. They were able to suck up about one liter of foul-tasting liquid from the "Seep" which Carl cheerfully described as "a muddy puddle filled with cow shit and covered with mosquito larvae," adding with a wide grin, "Isn't this great?!"

The next morning we set out for "Flint Seep," a red circle nine miles away according to the map. I rode in pain, oblivious to the spectacular views all around, focused on finding water. We reached the landmarks we had been looking for, a rock spire to the northwest and a double drainage. We dismounted and started searching. An hour later we were still looking for the water. Supposedly, there was a "spring" eleven miles away. However, we had no assurance it would be any easier to find. The oppressive desert sun beat down on us. Carl declared that "we must find Flint Seep!" Fifteen minutes later George discovered a mud puddle even less appetizing than the one from the previous night. We used the suction from compressing our bike water bottles to gain a few sips that we treated with double the recommended dose of iodine.

We pushed on for eleven miles where we found an animal trail leading to "French Spring," and clear, sweet water. We drank until we were sick, then drank again. We filled our bottles and headed out to explore the Mesas and Canyons. We rode to overlook an area appropriately called "The Maze." We circled a spectacular rock known as "Cleopatra's Chair." Finally we scrambled to the top of the highest formation on "Big Ridge" and enjoyed one of the most beautiful campsites of my life. Using French Spring as a central point for the next two days, we enjoyed some of the best riding and scenery in America and came to understand Carl's new mantra, "Live to ride, ride to die, mountain bikes from hell!" In retrospect "Hell Biking" was great. However, I do not think one needs to suffer to have an adventure. The next winter I contemplated a luxury trip.

"Neal, it'll be the ultimate luxury winter camping expedition! We'll traverse the Collegiate Range in Colorado supported by my friend Rick's dogsled team. The dogs pull three hundred pounds. We'll ski with light fanny packs. We'll climb all five fourteen-thousand-foot mountains and telemark down from their summits through pristine untracked powder. At night we'll stay in spacious dome tents with all the amenities of car camping. We'll have a charcoal grill, thick filet mignon, fresh fish, fine wines and great champagne . . ."

The more I talked about it, the better it sounded to me. Winter is my favorite time to explore America's wilderness areas. The backcountry of Yosemite, Yellowstone, the Tetons, and the Rocky Mountains is even more beautiful when laced with snow. There are no crowds. Cross country skiing adds an element of fun over plain hiking. By using sled dogs we'd ski unencumbered, climb the peaks, and even get a chance to do a bit of mushing ourselves. My team was perfect. Neal Beidleman is an aerospace engineer from Boulder, Colorado, a former professional ski racer and more importantly a gourmet chef. Rick Meinig is an orthopedic surgeon from Colorado Springs who races his team of huskies every weekend and prides himself on his German culinary skills. We decided to have a no-holds-barred high-altitude gastronomic competition.

When we began loading the sled I realized that I had made a couple of miscalculations. First, I didn't know that Rick rides on the dogsled with his gear. That meant we would have about two hundred pounds less carrying capacity than I anticipated. Neal did not have to be a rocket scientist to figure out how badly I fucked up. We packed as much as we could onto the sled, discarded nonessential items, and found ourselves with packs that were twice as heavy as what we would have carried for a lightweight winter camping expedition. Secondly, I forgot that January can be very cold at ten thousand feet in Colorado.

When Rick unloaded the dogs from his truck, our worries were temporarily forgotten. As soon as they saw the gear all six huskies began howling with delight and anticipation. Rick had to sink a steel anchor to prevent the sled from getting away. Those already in their harnesses strained against the weight until the others were ready. With a cry of "haw!" Rick released the anchor and the dogs screamed with joy. The sled quickly built momentum, and in less than three minutes topped the first rise and vanished from sight.

Our uplifted spirits were quickly deflated when we hoisted our packs. We trudged along with eighty pounds on our backs. There was no question of detours to climb the mountains above us. It took a maximal effort just to reach our campsite following the path of least resistance. As it was, we arrived after dark. Hours of uphill skiing had drained us, but Neal rallied to create a dinner of salmon, broccoli in a wine sauce, and couscous.

We had a final drink of hot chocolate and retired to our sleeping bags where Rick talked about mushing. "The name comes from the French, *marcher*, to march. But the dogs never march. They only have one speed, overdrive." Rick admitted that "you do have to be a little different to hassle with the dogs. But sledding cuts across all social barriers. The stereotype is my friend whom everyone calls Smelly. He has a big beard, wears a twelve-inch Bowie knife on his belt, and lives in a one-room trailer with about a hundred dogs. But there are also some mushers, like myself, who have jobs and families. I started with one dog and got such a kick having him pull me around on skis that I got another, and then another. During the summer I load them up with twenty pounds on dog packs. In winter the thrill of the speed and the enthusiasm of the team are just incredible. My wife, Kathy, is even starting to get better natured about it as long as I clean up the dogshit."

That night the temperature dropped. We didn't have a thermometer, but in Denver, where it averages forty degrees warmer, it was five below zero. The wine froze and the bottles cracked despite lying between our sleeping bags in the tent. The dogs woke excited to be alive for another great day of pulling. Neal and I were slightly less enthusiastic. The trip degenerated into a survival march. After humping maximum loads all day the last thing we wanted to do was stay outside and barbecue in the wind, even if the fish, meat, and everything else hadn't frozen solid.

Rick and his dogs did seem to be having fun, despite the temperatures, until the last afternoon when Rick threw a piece of food between his lead dog, Makalu, and a second dog called Devil. A fight broke out between the dogs. Rick rushed in to break it up and was bitten on his left forearm, down to the bone. After appropriate first aid we headed for home. The final leg was mostly downhill, my pack was lighter, and I was able to enjoy the magnificent scenery and think about the future. Safely back in the car I began describing my next ultimate trip. Neal cut me off: "Geoff, don't try and talk me into anything, ever again!"

The ultimate place for outdoor adventure in North America remains Alaska. There is still an incredible quantity of unexplored mountain territory, a wild coastline, and the highest peak on the continent, "Denali," the great one, as the Inuit call Mount McKinley. I climbed Denali working as a mountain guide, sharing the joy of a big mountain with novices. We flew from the small airstrip in Talkeetna, Alaska, to land on the snow runway of the Kahiltna International Airport, at eight thousand feet on the Kahiltna Glacier. We followed the West Buttress route. This path winds up low-angle snow slopes to a large campsite at fourteen thousand feet. From here, a short, steep section leads to a classic ridge that is followed to seventeen thousand feet. Above this, a moderate day of snow climbing brings us to the peak of North America. The technical difficulties of the climb are minimal, requiring only basic mountaineering abilities, crevasse safety techniques, winter camping skills and endurance. Yet, the beauty is equal to any range in the world. I enjoyed a perfect summit day with twenty-degree temperatures, no wind, and a cloudless sky to survey the view. It was made even better by sharing the summit with two excited clients who had become new friends and with my old friend, and fellow guide, Scott Woolems.

South America is another continent ripe for mountaineering adventures. Patagonia, at the Southern tip of Chile and Argentina, is one of the great areas of untamed mountain wilderness on earth. The Andes of Peru, Bolivia, Chile, and Argentina offer a wealth of high-altitude challenges, as do the volcanoes of Colombia and Ecuador. The Amazon Basin has plenty of hidden rock spires, and the city of Rio de Janeiro, Brazil, has the best urban rock climbing that I have encountered. My memories of climbing in South America are mostly joyous ones. However, I had one of my scariest nights in the mountains while guiding a climb in Bolivia.

I led a group from the Kenilworth Mountaineering Club on a climb of Mount Ilimani, an Andean giant that rises to twenty-one thousand feet from the altiplano outside of La Paz. It was a perfect trip, until summit day. I headed out from our high camp at the "Nido De Condores" roped to Frank "The Animal" Babb. Babb was a corporate attorney in his fifties who was delightful company; he was also able to push himself as hard as anyone I have met. I frequently asked Frank how he was doing as we climbed toward the summit. He always answered, "Just fine." I could tell that he was straining, but he kept up a reasonable pace and the weather seemed stable. We reached the summit just as Frank hit the wall.

Frank Babb had finished his marathon and collapsed. Clouds were rolling in from the other side of the peak. I pressed Frank to start down. He stood up, wobbled, and crumpled back down. I goaded him into descending with threats that he would never see his family again. Still, he was only able to manage a few paces before tumbling to the snow for a rest. A storm engulfed us when we were still above twenty thousand feet. I told Frank that we would have to bivouac and dug a trench into the side of a crevasse. Frank smiled at me gently and said, "Geoff, if those are our cards, I trust that you will play them right." Throughout the long night I was terrified that Frank would develop high-altitude cerebral or pulmonary edema and die, or that the storm would last several days and Frank would be too weak to descend and I would become too weak to carry him. Frank was paying me to keep him safe, and I had failed. Frank, meanwhile, remained cheerful and showed no signs of fear or serious illness. Fortunately, the weather improved the next morning and we descended safely. Reaching the "Nido De Condores" we were shocked to find the camp abandoned. There were no tents, and worse, no food, stove, or fuel left for us. When we failed to return the previous night, the other members of the club assumed we were dead. Early that morning they had left for La Paz to arrange for a helicopter to recover our bodies and to inform the world of our demise.

No such problems occurred on my climb of Cerro Aconcagua. I went to South America's highest peak with John Stetson, a wild man who trains sled dogs for a living and travels in the Arctic and Antarctic for fun. We hiked from Puenta de Inca, up the beautiful Horcones Valley, thirty-one kilometers, to a crowded international base camp where we enjoyed a festive New Year's Eve celebration in the company of crazed Australians. One of their group was a very beautiful, statuesque rock climber named Maureen Gallagher whom I had met climbing in Utah. I asked Maureen what she was doing on a big mountain, as I had always thought of her as a pure crag rat. She said she was expanding her horizons thanks to her "incredible new boyfriend, Jeffrey Little." I had heard of Jeffrey Little. Lydia Bradey, my friend from Everest, credited Jeff with transforming her as a climber and inspiring her to push her limits. Lydia also claimed that Jeff helped her set the world's high-altitude sex record, making love at twenty-five thousand feet on Gasherbrum. Having been to twenty-five thousand feet myself a few times and knowing how hard it was simply to breathe, let alone tie my shoes at that height, I was in awe of what a truly superhuman feat he had performed. I was excited to meet this mythical figure who had achieved a hero's status among several of my friends. Jeffrey Little turned out to be low-key with the physical appearance of a thin little Hobbit. Jeff stands less than five-feet-three-inches and has a long crooked nose and a balding head with blond hair cascading to his shoulders along the sides. From Maureen's adoring gaze and Lydia's stories, I surmised that he is much more than meets the eye.

Unfortunately, I did not get a chance to get to know Jeffrey well, as he went around the mountain to climb the South Face, while we headed up the North Ridge. Joining me and John on the trail to the top were Jim Morrissey, my Kangshung Face team leader, and his wife, Kathy. The "Ruta Normal" is basically a long hike, but with the altitude it can be a serious one. For me it was a happy reunion trip with friends. I again enjoyed a perfect sunny and calm day on the summit of South America.

Most of my European adventures took place in England and in the Alps. However, to climb the highest mountain on the continent one must go to the Caucasus Range. The Caucasus have a great variety of mountains that are perfect for climbers, skiers, and hikers. Moreover, with the changing politics of the former Soviet Union in 1990, it was a particularly exciting place to go to experience the awakening of the human spirit. The Soviet Union still existed, but was awash with political turmoil. I had wanted to visit the Caucasus since reading about Edward Whymper's adventures when I was in college.

I flew to Moscow with six friends who were going to share my seventh continental summit with me. Stu Ellison, Patrick Arbor, Don Palmer, Rich Neville, Morton Lane, Chris Hartley, and I all wanted to stand on the top of Europe together. We moved on to the Balkar Valley, on the other side of the Caucasus Mountains from Georgia, the land of yogurt-eating people who are renowned for remaining active well past the age of one hundred. The Balkarians claim that the Georgians are puny, weak, and die young. I was impressed with the number of wizened, gray-haired people loping rapidly and easily along the valley. While doing acclimatizing hikes from the Itkol Sport Hotel, I learned first-hand that the Balkarians also eat plenty of yogurt, with every meal. They also drink prodigious quantities of vodka. I wondered if the yogurt keeps these people strong and active until a very ripe age or if the vodka makes them look prematurely old.

We headed up to the Priut hut for our attempt at Mount Elbrus. The weather did not cooperate. We waited for the storms and high winds to ease. Unfortunately, several of my group had commitments back in America, and we began to run out of time. On the last possible day for us to climb the peak, we set out from the hut into a fierce wind. My team persevered up steep icy slopes until we all embraced on the windy summit at one o'clock in the afternoon of June 22, 1990. I thus became the fourth person, after Pat Morrow of Canada, Reinhold Messner of Italy, and Oswald Olz from Switzerland, in the seven summits club (counting Carstensz Pyramid as the highest in Australia/Oceana).

At our celebration back in Itkol one of our companions, Vladimir, suggested that Americans get old and fat very quickly. I pointed out that Pat Arbor had just climbed, in adverse conditions, to the highest point in Europe at age fifty-three. Vladimir countered that his uncle, Akhia Kochar, made the summit of Mount Elbrus, in much worse conditions, when he was eighty-four years old. I retorted that Patrick has a twenty-two-year-old girlfriend who seems very happy. Vladimir shot back, "When Uncle Akhia last climbed the mountain his girlfriend was nineteen!" After a brief pause he added, "and they just celebrated their forty-third wedding anniversary." When I expressed doubts, Vladimir led me to a toothless old man who walked without a cane. The old man produced a paper that Vladimir said was from the czar's army and proved Akhia was 127 years old. The document was faded, and written in Russian, so I'll never know for sure. However, after a couple more bottles of vodka, when we were all singing, I decided that it really didn't matter. We were all people who loved mountains and it was just great to be alive!

I have found that mountain people and adventurers are similar around the world. People who are willing to turn blind corners and accept challenges tend to be open minded about other aspects of life and have a wide-ranging curiosity. A remarkable number of my climbing partners have fueled their passion for life into other pursuits with remarkable success. This wide variety of accomplishment and mastery is exemplified by Louis Reichardt.

A Climber of Genius

IT'S A CHILLY EVENING in Yosemite Valley, and when Lou Reichardt and I arrive at the Mountain Room Bar after a day of climbing, the place is jammed. The party doesn't do much for Reichardt, who had attempted to skirt this evening by suggesting we stay in camp and eat Hershey bars for dinner. As we make our way through the crowd of mostly young, mostly color-coordinated climbers, you can't help but notice that the forty-six-year-old Reichardt is wearing a patched down coat, torn wool knickers, and thick, black-framed glasses held together by paper clips and tape. He looks like a theoretical scientist. He is.

"Look at Hubel's and Weisel's work on the importance of visual experience to normal cortex development," he tells me at the bar, commencing a forty-minute review of contemporary neurophysiology. That none of the nearby patrons add their two cents is no surprise. But you'd think somebody would at least recognize Dr. Louis French Reichardt, arguably America's foremost Himalayan mountaineer.

Reichardt has climbed three eight-thousand-meter peaks—a feat that only four other Americans, John Roskelley, Carlos Buhler, Ed Viesturs, and Chris Pizzo, have matched—and he's the first American to summit both Everest and K2. Moreover, he climbed Everest by way of the East Face—an approach considered suicidal from the time it was first surveyed in 1921, and reached the top of K2 without supplemental oxygen, another first. He's also thought to be the only climber to lug a backpack to the summit of Everest with the airline luggage tags intact, and the first to read *The Universe and Dr. Einstein* at twenty-seven thousand feet on K2.

Until recently, often upon the solution of some monstrous scientific problem, Reichardt would simply hang up his lab coat every three years or so and hike into the mountains to tackle something absurdly difficult. Months after he solved the long-standing mystery of how a cell differentiates itself, he climbed 26,810-foot Dhaulagiri. His widely applauded work on neuronal plasticity preceded an ascent of Nanda Devi, a climb so technically demanding that some characterized it as the best American effort in the Himalayas in nearly a decade.

But alas, Reichardt hasn't climbed a blessed thing for six years. Last year he scratched from an expedition up Kanchenjunga, the world's third-highest mountain, after learning that a research grant might be in jeopardy if he left. He's also passed on expeditions to Cho Oyu, Everest, Broad Peak, and the North Ridge of K2. Since climbing Everest in 1983, Reichardt's only adventures have been of the purely cerebral kind, in his neurology lab at the University of California, San Francisco. There, at the nether reaches of the in-vitro frontier, Reichardt lays one brain cell next to another and pursues his field's $64,000 question: Why do similar nerve cells sometimes grow and sometimes not? Why do they fail to regenerate after a spinal cord injury, yet succeed if the nerve damage is in an arm or leg?

Research in this area is still in its infancy, but Reichardt's previous accomplishments in both cellular biology and brain physiology—his resume runs to fourteen pages—have made him an academic superstar. "Lou is one of the leading researchers of his generation," says Zach Hall, chair of physiology at the University of California, San Francisco. Reichardt has been awarded two of science's most prestigious fellowships (the Guggenheim and the Howard Hughes), and he recently declined a deanship, an endowed professorship, and virtually unlimited research funds from Baylor Medical School. More than one colleague has mentioned him as a leading candidate for the Nobel prize. "If I hadn't lost so many brain cells to high-altitude hypoxia," he jokes, "I'd already have been to Stockholm."

Reichardt's long layoff from climbing, however, may be nearing an end. Several months ago, after learning that a National Institutes of Health grant would fund his lab through 1994, Reichardt pronounced himself ready again. "I am an incredibly fortunate person," he says. "If science and discovery are important to you, there could be no better job. But this is the time to go. I've never been this far from a grant proposal." The challenge of a climbing comeback could be overwhelming, but that's always been the draw for Reichardt. If there has been one clear pattern in his life, it has been his penchant for selecting outrageously difficult problems both in science and climbing. "What is exciting," he says, speaking of mountaineering but perhaps also of science, "is that the challenges almost always come from unexpected places." Would he start back with something moderate, a peak in South America, perhaps, or Alaska? "Maybe Namcha Barwa," he muses, electing a 25,445-foot Himalayan giant, the highest unclimbed peak in the world.

I first met Reichardt as his teammate on the 1981 and 1983 Everest East Face expeditions. When I saw him in San Francisco in 1989 I was impressed at how fit his six-foot-one, 180-pound frame appeared; it looked as though Reichardt had been confined to a gym, not the laboratory, for the last six years. Particularly formidable were his hulking forearms, ridged with thick veins and defined by a Harris Tweed jacket a size or two too small. I asked if he'd been working out. "I haven't had any physical exercise in years," he said, smiling. "I've been totally committed to science."

It's moments like these that make climbers wonder about Reichardt. His only regular training is a three-block walk to the bus stop and a one-flight stair-climb to his office, yet on expeditions, at severe altitude, he normally carries what seems to be twice the load at twice the speed of anyone else. Some say he must be a physiological freak, a person whose respiratory system is perfectly crafted for work at altitude; others contend that his mind simply drives his body past such niggling distractions as tedium, discomfort, and pain. Finally, there's the rumor that Reichardt *does* train—by spending long hours in his laboratory's cold-room. He denies it, but a co-worker claims to have discovered him in the room wearing only underwear.

Reichardt puzzles for other reasons: While other climbers clamor for donations of state-of-the-art equipment and mountaineering clothing, Reichardt prefers a 1969-issue backpack and a collection of hideous sun hats. He seeks no publicity. He's written no climbing books and just a few climbing articles, and he often mumbles about his deeds as if to make sure he'll never be quoted. ("I just wanted to, well, climb some things," he says of his summits of Dhaulagiri, Nanda Devi, K2, and Everest.) He says so little at times, but clearly knows so much, that it can be unsettling. "Lou is the smartest guy I've ever met, but we don't have much to talk about," says John Roskelley, who's been on four expeditions with Reichardt. Once, while waiting out a storm at 24,500 feet on Dhaulagiri, the pair didn't have a single conversation in ten days. "We weren't mad at each other," says Roskelley. "We just didn't have anything to say."

The same might be said by his scientific colleagues, few of who see the merit in risking one's life on a mountain or the logic of exposing a brain—especially Reichardt's brain—to potential damage from prolonged stays at altitude. On campus, a distracted Reichardt will often scoot right past acquaintances, responding to a bright hello with . . . nothing. Conversely, a joke from Reichardt is liable to leave lab folks pondering for days. "He has a very elliptical, highly condensed sense of humor," explains Zach Hall. "He'll say something, laugh, and then move along. It might be hours before you'll get the link he's made between disparate things. It's as if he's three steps ahead of everyone."

The son of a prize-winning architect and a housewife who later became a peace and civil rights activist, Lou Reichardt was born and raised in Pasadena, California. His parents, both avid backpackers, began taking him along on trips into the Sierra when he was ten. Soon, Reichardt says, "I was wandering off by myself, climbing anything that was nearby. I think it drove my parents nuts."

He attended Midland High School, a tiny, all-male boarding school near Los Angeles. "Lou was tall and awkward, with thick, greasy glasses," says Midland roommate, Joe Esherick, recalling his first impression. "No way, I thought, would he be athletic. But he was." Reichardt, Esherick, and a third classmate took a Sierra Club climbing course and made forays to nearby Taquitz Rock. "We were pretty unsophisticated," says Reichardt, an average beginner. "I remember this one long, crazy climb. It was before we started using nuts and things, and at one point I was sixty feet above my anchor. I had no business doing anything like that, but I finally made that damn thing. It made me appreciate the certain thrill in living beyond where someone should rationally live."

Perfect scores on his math SATs and his French boards earned Reichardt a National Merit Scholarship and a spot at Harvard in the fall of 1960. "It was kind of embarrassing," he says. "At Harvard they put me into third-year French. When I came to class they started reading poetry, and I didn't understand a word of it. It was clear I'd scored twice what I should have on the test." Reichardt intended to major in philosophy. ("I was never in high school science fairs or anything like that," he says. "I had endless ideas, but I could never get close to the finished product.") But he changed his mind soon after taking a class taught by James Watson, one of the discoverers of DNA. "The things he was saying were tremendously exciting. It was obvious that society was becoming driven by science."

He joined the renowned Harvard Mountaineering Club but never went on an expedition. "I had school to worry about, and I had to work in the summer," says Reichardt, who did fit in some rock climbing and tried ice climbing during summer vacations back in California.

In 1964 Reichardt went to Cambridge on a Fulbright scholarship, then to Stanford, where he first attacked the problem of how the myriad cells of a human body, all of which are genetically identical, differentiate to become muscle, nerve, bone, and blood. His academic elders considered the problem of gene expression far too complex for a Ph.D. candidate in physiology; Reichardt persisted anyway, taking the topic on in his doctoral thesis.

It was at Stanford that Reichardt got a reputation as a promising mountaineer and rock climber. He would unwind from an eighty-hour week in the lab by marching fifty miles in a weekend, typically climbing three ten-thousand-foot summits en route. His fortitude was spectacular, but there was perhaps no uglier stride in all of North America, the result of a college knee injury and his habit of taking one stride to anyone else's two. He also climbed in Yosemite with a Palo Alto crowd that included Paul Gerhard, one of the Bay Area's best climbers. Gerhard invited him on an expedition to Mount McKinley in 1967, the first of three trips they would take to Alaska.

The weather was unusually bad that year—six people died in a storm that kept most climbers from reaching the top—but Reichardt and Gerhard made it. "Mentally, going to McKinley was a much bigger step than going to the Himalayas," says Reichardt. "It was the first time I was really away from every-thing." Afterward Gerhard pushed to get Reichardt on a 1969 American team to Dhaulagiri. Three weeks before the team departed, a spot opened up for him. "I think I got to go because I was the only one without a real job," says Reichardt. "The Himalayas weren't really in my life plan."

The expedition went well at first. But on April 28, Reichardt was on the glacier beneath Dhaulagiri at 17,500 feet, taking photographs while his teammates worked to bridge a crevasse. Later he would write in his diary: "It began with the noise of an avalanche, then a mutual realization that it might hit us. Then there was silence. No screams, just silence. First came the real-ization that I was not hurt. It couldn't have been that bad. Then came the discovery that nothing was there—no tents, no cache, no ice axe, and no friends. A moment of hope. It was just a snow avalanche. Hey, Boyd! Hey, Dave! Hey, Vin! I'm alive and OK; here to dig you out. Just let me know where you are. No answers."

Reichardt performed two exhaustive searches—first by him-self and later with the expedition members who had been at base camp at the time of the avalanche—but no bodies were recovered. Seven of the finest climbers in the world were dead.

By a quirk of fate, Reichardt, who had been in the middle of them moments before, was left to tell the story. He returned to America and traveled from San Francisco to Connecticut to visit the friends and families of the victims. "I wasn't ready to go back to the research," he says. "I was pretty blown away."

Reichardt resumed his graduate work several months later and published *Regulation of Repressor Synthesis and Early Gene Expression by Bacteriophage and Lambda Virus* in 1972. The dissertation provided a model to explain how one cell develops differently from the next. The understanding of gene expression was radically altered by Reichardt's work, and today it is one of the basics in any medical school curriculum. "I think all of my promotions and appointments still come from my dissertation," he says. "It's the only really important thing I've done." Hall, along with others, thought it worthy of Nobel consideration.

In 1973, Reichardt went back to Dhaulagiri with another strong team. Many climbers were stunned to hear that he was returning to the mountain where he had witnessed one of American climbing's worst tragedies. "Lou carried the heaviest loads, pushing hard day after day," says Roskelley, who was amazed by Reichardt's strength and intensity. Teammate Jim Morrissey remembers a day when he and Reichardt hiked into base camp. Subtly, they both accelerated the tempo, turning the trek into something of a race. It ended in a dead heat. The next day, while hiking at sixty-five hundred feet, they learned that a teammate had cerebral edema at fourteen thousand feet. They took off, and at eleven thousand feet Morrissey doubled over sick. As his partner raced on, Morrissey asked, "God, Lou, how can you keep going?" Reichardt put it this way: "Mind over matter."

They pushed on to 24,500 feet and waited out a storm for ten days; then, well into the so-called death zone where the body begins to deteriorate from lack of oxygen, Reichardt and Roskelley bulled their way to the summit without supplemental oxygen. On the way down, Reichardt's suspenders snapped and his thick glasses fogged; in a kind of Himalayan Charlie Chaplin skit, his pants fell to his knees whenever he reached up to wipe his glasses. He also suffered a mild case of ataxia, a loss of coordination and sense of balance. Though Morrissey offered help, mostly he observed in bemused wonder as Reichardt stubbornly marched into base camp under his own power, tail bared to the wind. There, Reichardt diagnosed his ataxia as resulting from a minor stroke in the cerebellum. At that moment, it occurred to him, his vocation and avocation were for the first time in perfect harmony.

"In mountaineering there's real discovery, pushing of limits," says Reichardt, who counts Dhaulagiri, his first Himalayan peak, as his favorite. "You live on the edge, figuring out what you need to do to stay on the right side of the line. Science is sort of similar."

In fact, when he returned from Dhaulagiri, life on another edge—the scientific edge—was foremost in Reichardt's mind. "After my dissertation, I could have coasted," he says. "I could have stayed in cellular biology for the rest of my life or go into something new and wild. I decided to go into neurological biology even though I didn't know much about it. It was considered really far-out, the wildest type of biology there was. It was a risk—I might not have ended up under an avalanche, but I could have been left without a grant, which is scientific death."

As it turned out, Reichardt made the right decision, producing brilliant work as a postdoctoral fellow at Harvard from 1974 to 1976 and attracting job offers from the major research centers and universities across the country. He put them all off—at least for the summer—and went to India instead.

The infamous Nanda Devi expedition was a tortured one from start to finish, culminating in the tragic death of co-leader Willi Unsoeld's twenty-one-year-old daughter. Reichardt generally stayed out of the number of squabbles that afflicted the expedition and partly for that reason was elected climbing leader. He toiled at shepherding the large, feuding team up the 25,645-foot mountain, and eventually he, Roskelley, and Jim States—each carrying seventy-five pounds of gear over the route's most difficult section, a thousand-foot sheer vertical buttress beneath the summit area—pushed to Camp Four. When it was time to summit a few days later, Reichardt balked. According to his altimeter, the trio had fifteen hundred feet to go; it was already midday, and if the altimeter was accurate, they'd probably have to bivouac without any gear. Reichardt trusted the reading and wanted to retreat. The others refused. Against his better judgment, Reichardt made the ascent. The three summitted at 2 P.M. on September 1, returned to camp before dark, and proved Reichardt wrong about the altimeter and right about his theory: The beauty of an expedition begins when things start to screw up.

Harvard, MIT, and Cal Tech had offered posts to Reichardt back in the spring, but only the University of California, San Francisco, agreed to let him take prolonged leaves of absence to climb. "He was the first person I hired," says Zach Hall, who started the university's neuroscience program, now regarded as one of the best in the country. Hall signed Reichardt on the strength of his Harvard work—he had pioneered a technique to distinguish among the many types of brain cells, allowing the neuroanatomists to study rare populations of neurons—but the two had been friends since meeting at Stanford in 1967.

"His stamina is amazing," says Hall. "His style has never been slick or graceful, but he has this tremendous ability to focus his energies and get things done, to cut right through to what's important." The parallels to his climbing style are unmistakable. Reichardt has often said that when he's on the mountain he thinks of nothing but climbing, and when he's in the lab, nothing but science. Nothing. When climbing with him, it's not unusual to have to holler simply to capture his attention. "He'll appear oblivious sometimes," says Hall, "but it's more that he's recognized that what's going on is not important."

In 1978, an American expedition was gathering for an assault on K2. Americans had been trying to climb the world's second-highest mountain since the 1930s, and though Reichardt was at the crux of his new research, he couldn't say no.

The Karakoram Range suffered from a series of terrible storms in 1978. As the American group trekked in, they met a beleaguered British expedition that had already given up on K2.

The Americans went on, changing strategy daily on account of the weather. Reichardt was again the pacesetter. "Without him, we probably would have turned back," expedition member Rick Ridgeway wrote later. When it came time to make a summit bid, Reichardt's oxygen system failed and he fell behind Jim Wickwire, his summit partner. He discarded the seventeen-pound unit, dumped his pack and parka, and caught Wickwire just below the summit. "Tell me if I exhibit any bizarre behavior," said Reichardt, worried that the lack of oxygen would impair his judgment. A short time later the pair walked onto the 28,250-foot summit. "He lacked what, to the rest of us, was the main limiter of our efforts; feedback from the body to the mind," Ridgeway wrote. "Lou's body just carried out the mind's orders."

Lou Reichardt is at the helm of the family mini-van, calmly piloting his four children home from a church dinner. In the back seat, Anna, Ben, Christian, and Isa, ages four to twelve, are attempting to lever a heavy pack up to the front seat. Cries of "Louie! Louie!" drown out conversation. Seven-year-old Ben begins to scale the front seat when Reichardt spies him in the rearview mirror. "Now Ben, it is imperative that you remain stationary and fasten your seat belt," he says. By the time the Reichardt clan arrives at its modest stucco home in the hills overlooking the Cal-San Francisco Medical Center, the noise has approached the supersonic.

Reichardt's wife, Kathy, is away this afternoon, and he valiantly attempts to attend to a visitor as the four precocious youngsters spread out. Outside in the driveway, one has inexplicably dropped a rotten Halloween pumpkin on the hood of Reichardt's Toyota truck. Inside, Isa confronts her dad. "Louie," lectures the twelve-year-old, "you have already inflicted severe psychological damage by missing my birthday. Don't you think it would be a mistake to miss my school play?" Reichardt agrees that it would.

These days Reichardt is much more reluctant to take large chunks of time away from his wife and children. "My first priority is my family," says Reichardt, who rarely goes anywhere socially without the gang. "Ever since I became a father, I'm not as willing to stick my neck out."

There are occasional exceptions to this rule, such as Reichardt's trip to Everest in 1981. Hidden in Tibet, the mountain's East Face is its largest and steepest side. It was first seen by Western climbers during the 1921 British Everest Reconnaissance, when George Leigh-Mallory declared it to be unclimbable, concluding that "other men, less wise, might attempt this way, but emphatically it was not for us." The British moved around to the north, where all subsequent Tibetan assaults on the mountain took place.

But in 1981 the Chinese sold Americans a permit to make the first climbing attempt on the East Face, and Reichardt was named the climbing leader. The standard expedition bickering soon erupted into open warfare. Unaccustomed to the role of massaging overamped egos and disinclined to referee the disputes, Reichardt instead showed his leadership by hefting double loads up the mountain. His understated diplomacy failed, and six climbers, including Roskelley, abandoned the effort. Some on the expedition suggested an easier route, but on that subject Reichardt was uncompromising. "There is no greater challenge for a climber than an untested face," Reichardt once said, and clearly he had no intention of substituting anything less demanding. The handicapped squad did find a route up the initial forty-five-hundred-foot sheer buttress but stalled from lack of support at twenty-two thousand feet.

Reichardt returned to the East Face in 1983, so determined to climb it that he had actually run "up to five miles in a single day," worked out on pull-up bars, and squeezed a grip exerciser. Led by Jim Morrissey, veteran American alpinist George Lowe, and Reichardt, the team quickly worked their way up the mountain. When it came time to choose a summit team, Reichardt was picked along with Carlos Buhler and Kim Momb. Equipment problems delayed Reichardt on the morning of the summit push, and he was forced to climb hurriedly to catch his partners. He finally tracked them down, six hours later, where the East Face merges with the southeast summit ridge at 27,500 feet. From there, Reichardt broke trail through deep snow all the way to the south summit. For the sake of speed, the trio climbed without a rope, knowing what a slip on the exposed ridge would mean. At two o'clock in the afternoon, thirteen hours after leaving camp, Reichardt, Momb, and Buhler completed the first ascent of the East Face. "Nobody ever believes this, but I never go on any of my trips expecting to reach the summit," says Reichardt, who has been the first to the summit each time one of his expeditions landed someone on top. "In the case of Everest, I'd never in my life dreamed I'd actually get up the thing."

Reichardt's strength on Everest gave rise to still more theorizing about how he could be so good at altitude. Reichardt disputed the notion that he is some kind of genetic freak uniquely adapted for high-altitude work. "One of the first times I went high, I had a terrible case of altitude sickness," he says. "I was dehydrated when I started the climb, and forgot to bring a water bottle. I had a splitting headache and dry heaves."

Reichardt knows that less oxygen in the air can be compensated for by deeper, more rapid breathing. But faster breathing means you exhale more, losing moisture and acid. Your blood becomes alkaline, a problem that the kidneys deal with by selectively excreting alkaline urine and saving acid. Together, the heavy breathing and the kidneys' compensatory mechanism lead to dehydration. Old climbers' lore holds that at altitude you should "drink until your piss is gin-clear."

Reichardt lives by this rule. "On Everest, I never saw him without a water bottle in his hand," says Buhler. Proper hydration is one part of Reichardt's systematic, ever-logical approach to altitude. He starts his daily carries of supplies before dawn and pushes himself to go twice as fast as most climbers in order to finish his chores early. He then spends the rest of the day melting snow to drink, making sure to shield his head from the high-altitude sun. Never one for small talk, he eschews most expedition socializing to rest in his tent. He often forces down huge gulps of high-calorie food with his liquid, even if he's not hungry. On Everest, Carl Tobin says, it wasn't uncommon to see Reichardt stuff four or five Almond Roca candy bars into already-bulging cheeks. Reichardt says this regimen of maximal exertion followed by concentrated drinking, eating, and rest allows him to work hard each day. And that when it's time for a summit bid, he's both acclimatized and fit.

Reichardt's climbing partners remain unconvinced that it's as simple as he makes it sound. "Lou is a thoroughbred at altitude," says Roskelley. "Put him on a mountain and it's like he was born to run." Physiological research supports that notion. People who acclimatize best to altitude breathe harder and faster when the oxygen content in their blood drops even a little bit. That explains why marathon runners, who endure maximal exertion with a minimum of huffing and puffing, often fare poorly at altitude. Reichardt, who sprinted in high school, breathes heavily with the slightest exertion, even at sea level, giving the impression that he's horribly out of shape. To the contrary, his overactive respiratory response combines with what must be a genetically humongous lung capacity to make him superior at altitude.

Jim Morrissey, a partner on five expeditions, has another theory: "Lou is unstoppable, not because of physiology, but because of attitude. He's one of the most powerful, capable, and determined mountaineers in the world because he's more focused and driven than anyone else. He also has an incredibly high pain threshold." Says Reichardt: "Science and climbing are intellectual exercises. There are specific things in each that you just suffer through."

Reichardt's laboratory is awash in centrifuges, microscopes, and science journals. He supervises a dozen graduate students and postdoctoral fellows, who daily, from eight o'clock A.M. to eight o'clock P.M., try to discover what makes nerve cells live or die. It is new scientific territory. "This is like cancer research ten years ago," Reichardt says of the ongoing struggle to understand the human brain. "It's intense, but the pressures aren't the same as on expeditions, where people will literally hate each other. People aren't scared in the same way."

"Basically, my job is to figure out how things work, to try and think of good ideas, raise new questions. The stuff I do in the lab is in some ways not so different from, say, the problem of how to get two food bags from Camp Two to Camp Four."

In the six years since Everest, Reichardt's mind has been exclusively devoted to science. Early in his tenure at Cal-San Francisco Medical Center, he did pioneering work with nerve growth factors, the proteins that decide whether neurons live or die. Their existence was cause for much optimism in the scientific community. If scientists could stimulate nerve cells to grow, they could regenerate damaged brain tissue. "Most solutions are only half-solutions," Reichardt cautions about the immense problem before him. The research could occupy a lifetime, maybe much longer, which may be why Reichardt is ready to go climbing again. "One reason he likes to climb," says Kathy Reichardt, "is that when you climb a mountain, the problem is either done or not done."

Since 1983, Reichardt's work-and-family schedule has allowed for exactly one weekend of rock climbing each year. Still, nobody doubts his ability to knock off another Himalayan giant, be it Kanchenjunga or Namcha Barwa. Even with the long respite, he has spent more time above twenty-four thousand feet than any other American. And at forty-six, he isn't unusually old for a Himalayan climber, many of whom reach their prime in their thirties, even early forties. "If you can climb one," he says, "you should be able to climb them all." Reichardt may again prove his mastery over both science and climbing, but that isn't ultimately what he cares to be known for. "My goal is to have children who remember me fondly," he says, the dizzying complexities of two brilliant careers unerringly simplified to the most obvious and important of responsibilities. "There is nothing that gives me more pleasure than being with my children."

Last spring, Reichardt returned to Yosemite for a full week. The object was to relax, but there was something else to do, too. Twelve-year-old Isa Reichardt had told her father she wanted to climb Mount Rainier. He agreed to lead her up the mountain if she met his criteria: First, she would have to hike an advanced trail in Yosemite. Next would come a climb of Mount Shasta, which would reveal her capability on snow and ice. Finally, she'd have to summit Mount Whitney, California's highest peak, to determine how she fared at altitude. While the park burst with early spring dogwood and a thousand waterfalls, Reichardt timed his daughter as she hiked up to the Yosemite Falls Trail. He reports that she knocked off the three miles and twenty-seven hundred vertical feet in well under the allotted time. Mount Shasta is next. Though the preparation may seem excessive to Isa, she should be thankful. They could be going to the cold-room.

KAY GUARNAY

FIVE DAYS AFTER DAWA TSERING, NIMA TASHI, Phu Dorje, Peggy Luce, and I stood together on the summit of Mount Everest, Nima Tashi said to me in halting English, "Dr. Geoff come Pangboche, O.K.?"

"Why?"

"My wife has baby," he replied, his head bobbing from side to side.

"When?"

"I think today."

We raced down from base camp to Pangboche, covering in six hours what took us three days to trek up. Arriving at his two-story stone and wood home, we rushed inside before I had a chance to catch my breath. The lower floor housed his animals. We pushed past a goat and two small yaks and climbed upstairs to the smoky living area. Nima Tashi motioned for me to sit down on the long wooden bench that lined the wall next to the wood-burning cooking area. The opposite wall had shelves filled with large copper pots, expedition sleeping bags, stuff sacks, and a small shrine with a *thanka* painting and a small statue of Buddha. The center of the single-room house was empty except for three wooden columns supporting the carbon-stained ceiling.

We were immediately attended to by a slender Sherpani. She filled both our glasses to the rim with home-brewed *chang*, then pushed mine to my lips, admonishing me to drink. "Shay-shay-shay." After every sip my glass would be refilled, and I would be urged to drink again. Relief from the forced consumption of alcohol came only when she went to cook potatoes and a hot chili sauce for us. After several minutes I asked, "Nima Tashi, is this your wife?"

"Yes."

"I thought she was having a baby?"

"Yes."

"When?"

"Three hours ago."

We stepped over to the pile of yak wool blankets on the sleeping portion of the bench on the other side of the stove. Sleeping peacefully in the covers was a newborn girl.

That evening most of the village crowded into Nima Tashi's home. Everyone brought offerings of "Kata," blessed silk scarves, and *chang*. Dawa Tsering and Phu Dorje came down for the party. We celebrated the birth of a baby and the four of us reaching the top of Chomolungma and returning. Four generations of warmth glowed in the dim candlelight. People began singing and then dancing. The Sherpas locked arms, singing the melody and giving the beat with an intricate series of steps that resonated on the wooden floor. I joined in the dance line, swaying from the drink, unable to pick up the steps and only avoiding crashing onto my face from the support of Sherpa friends holding me by the shoulders. Turning to Dawa Tsering, I slurred, "Someday you must come celebrate in America."

Two weeks later, at Namche Bazaar, I said good-bye to my Sherpa friends. Dawa Tsering headed for his home in Gumella, a poor village with a population of thirty, three days' walk away. As a child, Dawa spent a year in Khumjung going to school but had to quit at age seven to work as a porter and yak herder. Now, as a top climbing Sherpa, he owned six yaks and a small plot of land where he hoped to build his own house. Our expedition over, I thought Dawa planned to see his parents and then join a French trekking group.

The American members of our team flew from Lukla to Katmandu, where we spent a week celebrating and tying up expedition business. On our last day in Nepal I found Dawa Tsering waiting at our hotel holding a vinyl carry-on bag less than half full.

"Dawa!" I greeted him. "I thought you were trekking with the French?"

"I go America with you," he said with an even smile. "You say, come see my family, O.K.,'" he added, bobbing his head from side to side.

"Dawa, do you have a passport?"

"Passport?" Dawa's face was blank.

"Do you have a visa?"

"Visa?"

We found an interpreter who explained to Dawa that he needed special papers to visit America. I called the U.S. Embassy and was assured that with a letter from me, my summit partner could have a visa to visit America. However, they cautioned, it is very difficult for Buddhist Sherpas to obtain passports from the Hindu-dominated government. When the translation was finished, Dawa smiled and quietly said, "Kay guarnay." I promised Dawa that if he got a passport and visa I would buy him a plane ticket. We parted with hugs and smiles at the Katmandu airport.

Dawa had shown no outward signs of disappointment. He had given up a lucrative trekking job and walked for eight days from his home to the nearest road, where he took a crowded, bumpy bus to Katmandu; only to find out he could not come to America. "Kay guarnay." Unless one spends a great deal of time with Sherpas it is difficult to comprehend their complacency at times like this. Once again the four essential truths came to mind: man suffers, suffering is caused by unfulfilled desire, overcoming desire eliminates suffering, and to eliminate desire you must follow the eight-fold path to wisdom. They do not preach this way of life. The Sherpas just live it.

The Sherpas migrated from Tibet to the highlands of Nepal some five hundred years ago. They number about six thousand, all of whom share the same last name—Sherpa. In addition to cultivating the high fields and raising yaks, the Sherpa people traditionally worked as traders, carrying goods between Nepal and Tibet over the high passes. The British hired Sherpas as porters for the first reconnaissance of Everest in 1921 and were amazed by their strength at altitude and mountaineering talent. Moreover, they are a delight to be with. Sherpa people have now accompanied so many expeditions that the term "Sherpa" has become synonymous with the job of high-altitude porter.

Three months after returning to the United States I received a telex: "Mr. Dawa Tsering Sherpa has visa and passport and awaits ticket to your home." Two days later Dawa took his first airplane ride—Katmandu to Delhi, Delhi to Singapore, Singapore to Los Angeles.

At the Los Angeles airport Dawa was to be met by my climbing friend David Dossetter and his wife, Susan. Two hours after all other passengers had cleared customs, Dawa was still nowhere to be seen. Worried, Dave spoke to an official. A short search revealed a Sherpa sitting quietly on a bench in the luggage area. He had with him just his small vinyl carry-on bag, a passport, no money, and less than a hundred words of English. Dave and Susan took Dawa directly from the airport to Disneyland, where Goofy's fiftieth birthday party was in full swing. Dawa ascended "Space Mountain" for a roller coaster ride and swing danced with Minnie Mouse on Main Street beneath the fireworks. That evening he attended a black-tie party in Bel Aire, complete with a sushi chef on the lawn. He had barely five hours of sleep before scoping the outdoor brunch scene amidst roller-skating grannies and steroid muscle men on Venice Beach. Susan later told me, "We wanted to show Dawa as much of California as we could. I was amazed. Nothing seemed to surprise him. He laughed a lot at Disneyland. Otherwise, it was as if he did these things every day. He's so calm."

That night Dawa flew to Chicago's O'Hare airport, where I picked him up. He had no plans or expectations other than that he was going to live with me for two months. Having already spoken to Dave, I excitedly asked, "Did you like Los Angeles?"

"Yes."

"What did you like best?"

"Susie is very nice."

Initially Dawa accompanied me wherever I went. He always tried to pick up on what was going on and help out whenever he could, insisting on carrying any packages that I had. No one ever questioned his following me into the emergency room, wearing a green scrub suit and carrying my medical bag. When I had to leave him alone he was seemingly content to watch videos or the television, even though his English was not sufficient to follow most conversations. His favorite movie was *E.T.*, which he watched a dozen times with joy. Whatever was offered, he always smiled and said, "It's O.K." with a little bob of his head.

I finally asked Dawa what he wanted to see or do while he was in America. "Maybe, work for money?" he replied.

It was not easy finding employment in Chicago for a man without a green card whose only proven skills are herding yaks, building stone fences, and carrying heavy loads up steep mountains. We tried a fancy restaurant called the "Everest Room" to see if they wanted a Sherpa greeter who had been up Everest, but received a firm no from the stuffy manager.

Eventually we found a man who installed aluminum siding. He hired Dawa for minimum wage but gave him a raise after one week. His employer said that he did the work of three people. Dawa soon found a second job as a busboy in a restaurant. In two months he made more money in America than he made in a year as a top climbing Sherpa in Nepal.

As Dawa and I became better friends and his English improved, he slowly revealed more of himself to me. He was surprised that I regularly asked him how he liked his jobs or what he thought of things.

"Things are what are." And he would shrug.

To Dawa, America was not better or worse, only different. This contrasted sharply with my own Western judgmental mind. He saw change in Nepal the same way. My American friends and I *judged* the changes that we thought we saw in Nepal. Dawa said we did not understand. More tourists in the Khumbu were not bad or good, they just were. "Kay guarnay." More money, better medical care, and schools are balanced against the erosion and garbage. "Kay guarnay."

There was no hint of jealousy, envy, or pity as I observed America through Dawa's eyes. One of Dawa's favorite finds in America was running water. He enjoyed taking a hot shower, or turning on the tap for a cool drink. With the money he made in America Dawa planned to start building his house in Gumella. He happily told me that his land was only a ten-minute walk, up a hill, from a river.

There were, of course, certain things that impressed even an accepting Buddhist mind. The glitzy, high tech, and luxurious aspects of Western life did not fascinate him as much as strange creatures, like big fish. At the Shedd Aquarium Dawa pressed his face against the first tank with a wide-eyed look. He began laughing and shaking his head. After fifteen minutes I grabbed his arm to drag him to the next exhibit. He held his ground laughing and then turned to me saying, "Fish like goat, as big as goat." I succeeded in getting him to the next tank where giant turtles had an equal effect. The next weekend we went to the Lincoln Park Zoo. Dawa had heard legends of big animals when he was growing up, but this was beyond his imagination. He particularly liked the African elephants, giraffes, and hippos. He also was happy to see the yaks in the zoo, a bit of home. And the size of the buildings impressed the man of the Himalayas. I tried to get permission for Dawa and me to walk the stairs to the top of the Sears Tower so that we could climb both the highest mountain and tallest building together. After wasting several hours with various building officials we settled for the elevator. Dawa said the view from the top of the tower was "the best."

Nothing fazed Dawa. He seemed happy in every setting, until we went to the Chicago Lyric Opera to see *Salome*. First, he did not like having to wear a tie. He asked me why everyone in America wears them. I could think of no good answer but still insisted he wear one. The music he found fine. But, when they brought out John the Baptist's head on a silver platter, Dawa turned to me and said, "I think we must go now, O.K."

The opera was one of only two times that Dawa appeared uncomfortable. The other occurred a few nights later when, in an attempt to expose Dawa to the breadth of American experience, my friend Bruce Goldstick and I took him to a Jello Wrestling night at a biker bar on Chicago's Northwest Side. A ring with three feet of foam rubber was covered by a slick plastic tarp which was coated with oil and then two feet of Jello cubes. Four girls came out and did striptease dances, down to G-strings. Each had her own distinctive wrestling motif like "Machine Gun Molly" or "Amazon Annie." Then the matches began. The combatants attempted to duplicate the moves of professional wrestlers on television, but basically just slipped around in the Jello. The emcee, a comedian, announced the bouts and insulted the men in the audience. Dawa sat in the front row, mesmerized by the action. The emcee announced that an auction would be held for a man to wrestle the girls.

Before the final match I spoke to the emcee, gave him a bribe and begged for a short intercontinental match with Dawa Sherpa. He agreed. After Machine Gun Molly won, the loudspeaker announced, "We have a special event. A three-minute match between our champion and Mr. Sherpa, who trains by climbing Mount Everest!" The spotlight turned to Dawa. I sensed the same fear in him that I felt when I first confronted the Khumbu Icefall.

Dawa dove under the table, hugging my leg saying, "NO! NO! NO!" It took several minutes of coaxing by Bruce, Molly, and me before Dawa agreed to go. He was led to the changing room by a typical bouncer at a rough motorcycle bar: six-feet-six-inches tall with a big gut and a face that looked like it had taken its share of crowbars. I still don't know exactly what Dawa thought was going to happen when this giant brought him into a back room and told him to strip. However, the thin, five-foot-three-inch Sherpa bolted, wide-eyed, from the room. He picked the bouncer up and threw him out of the way before dashing back to our table. The bouncer crashed through a table like a stunt man in a Western movie. A wave of terror spread over me. But, before the hulk could get up, the emcee had the whole crowd chanting, "Sherpa! Sherpa! Sherpa!"

It took another ten minutes of cajoling to finally get Dawa to enter the ring, fully clothed, and square off against a bikini-clad Machine Gun Molly. Dawa stood, looking confused. Molly rushed him, bouncing off and slipping away as Dawa firmly kept his footing. On her fourth try she knocked him off balance. Dawa picked her up and threw her onto the mat. The crowd erupted into new chants of, "Sherpa! Sherpa! Sherpa!" A lifetime of Buddhist pacifism melted away as Dawa Tsering Sherpa began to attack. He picked Molly up above his head and hurled her down into the muck. Two other girls came into the ring and were body slammed, airplane spun, and pinned as the crowd went into a frenzy. Dawa was declared the Intercontinental Intergender Wrestling Champion of the World.

Before he returned to Nepal we had a farewell party for Dawa. He cooked a big Nepal dinner and tried brewing *chang*. The dinner was great—spicy curry, hot chili sauce, and mo-mos. However, the *chang* didn't work, so I bought vodka and sake, mixed them together and told everyone it was *chang*. I pressed it to Dawa's lips, saying, "Shay-shay-shay." Everyone got a little drunk and Dawa was his most talkative ever in English.

Dawa said he was going home to start building his house in Gumella before the spring climbing season. He was also scheduled to marry during the monsoon. It was arranged by his father. He had only seen the girl once.

We discussed love and lust for a while before I asked, "Dawa, will you marry her?"

"Kay guarnay!" he replied. Of course. He must marry her.

People at the party asked Dawa if he liked his stay in America. He quietly bobbed his head and said yes. When pressed on what his favorite things were in America, Dawa said, "Many people are nice." He was then asked if he would like to stay longer. "I must go."

My mother gave Dawa Tsering a gift as we prepared to drive to the airport. She then asked him, "Dawa, what will you miss the most about America when you are back in Nepal?"

Dawa paused for a moment, smiled broadly, and said, "I think Jello wrestle."

Death

RETURNING FROM AFRICA, in 1990, I had a three-hour layover in London's Heathrow airport. I was walking through the terminal when I saw a familiar picture in a newspaper. It was a large photograph of Giles Kershaw. I excitedly went and bought a copy of the paper and turned to the page, expecting to read of some new heroics performed by the great Antarctic aviator. It was an obituary.

The reality is that adventure can be dangerous. Ten of my friends mentioned previously in this book have already died. Giles crashed a gyrocopter in Antarctica. Kim Momb and John Rutt were caught in avalanches in Canada. Dave Cheesmond and Mugs Stump perished in separate climbing accidents in Alaska. Peter Boardman fell high on the Northeast Ridge of Mount Everest. Charlie Shertz was buried in a slide on Manaslu in Nepal. Phu Dorje Sherpa fell to his death descending from the South Summit of Mount Everest after his second ascent of the mountain. Jean Marc Boivin crashed parachuting in Venezuela. And Dan Reid died with his wife, Barbara, in a fall from Mount Kenya.

In the wake of these tragedies and the carnage on Mount Everest in 1988 I was surprised and saddened by several strong statements about Americans not pushing the frontiers in world climbing. In particular, our 1988 ascent of Everest came under criticism for following an established route, using Sherpa climbers to help with the load carrying, and using bottled oxygen. My feeling is that these criticisms are unfounded, misleading, and do not understand the nature of adventure as a personal quest. Several Americans are still pushing the limits of what is currently possible. But the question of just how far the limits should be pushed remains unanswered.

Talk to Carlos Buhler about how strung out he was on the world's third highest peak, or shake Ed Webster's left hand and feel what he lost in Tibet. When Eric Escoffier raced up K2 a few years ago he was hailed as a hero, despite the fact that his partner died on the descent. When Peter Bozik (who died on Everest in 1988) climbed the "Magic Line" on K2, it was hailed as a great breakthrough, even though one of his partners died. Will anyone call Josef Just's ascent of the Southwest Face of Everest, on which he died, a victory?

Every climber should feel free to decide how close to the edge he wants to push. For me, no mountain is worth a life, no route a finger or toe. Perhaps our expedition in 1988 was out of touch with the trend toward light and fast ascents in the Himalayas: we used oxygen and climbed an easier route. But we also succeeded and brought everyone home in excellent health. I could not personally have reached the summit without my teammates and Sherpa friends. Their support only increased my pleasure in the experience. Going up the "standard" route was steep, exciting, and fun, and it was a great personal adventure for me. And that is at the core of why I climb.

Considering the death toll on Everest in 1988 and on K2 in 1986, perhaps we climbers should think again about what is important in mountaineering. The death rate among the best climbers attempting state-of-the-art ascents above eight thousand meters has reached an unacceptable level. Another major problem is that with multiple permits being given out for the same routes, numerous teams now swarm over the world's biggest peaks. This increases the danger and diminishes the experience for everyone, and will certainly lead to more political and safety problems in the future. Unfortunately, the issue of granting permits is out of the climber's control.

But we do have control over how we choose to climb. Despite the number of firsts, and the records, my vote for the top billing in the 1988 circus on Everest goes to Johnny Petroske and Steve

Ruoss, who gave up their summit attempt to save the life of a fellow climber. To me, that is what being a real mountaineer is all about.

And Dan Reid was what being a human being is all about. He truly maximized every moment of his existence on earth. He cared for his fellow creatures and freely shared his love and skills with those of us fortunate to have met him.

Dan Reid—A Life

THE BODIES OF DAN AND BARBARA REID were found in late September 1991 at the base of the ice window route on Mount Kenya. No one knows exactly what happened. There was a storm and they separated from the other rope team. Barb was on her first technical climb on a big mountain as part of her fortieth birthday celebration. Dan had not climbed in eight years. Yet, it still seems inconceivable that Dan Reid died in the mountains, or died at all. I expected him to call me to join him in adventures when he was a hundred years old. He died a few weeks before his fiftieth birthday, looking half his age, but having lived more than any three people twice as old. Reid lived life on his own terms, with unbridled enthusiasm and full-throttle pedal to the metal overdrive at all times. He did not simply march to the beat of a different drummer, he sprinted to the sounds of his own bagpipe orchestra.

I met Dan on the East Face of Mount Everest where he was a doctor on the first American climbing expedition into Tibet in 1981. The slight, bespectacled, cardiac surgeon was supposed to be our base camp physician. However, he moved onto the steep initial buttress to belay George Lowe when others demurred because of the weather. Later Reid attempted to solo an icicle at twenty-one thousand feet on a day too nasty for even Lowe to leave his tent. No matter that Reid had never attempted to climb vertical ice before. He self-belayed on three forty-foot whippers on "Reid's Nemesis" before giving up. A few days afterward a falling rock hit Reid as he was descending an ice gully known as the "Bowling Alley." He received an implosion injury exposing his tibia. It required thirty-eight stitches to close the wound. Two weeks later, after the rest of the team retreated, Dr. "PercoDan," popped some of his own medications and headed up the ropes, vanishing into a cloud. He descended after thirty-six hours of continuous climbing. With a big grin he said "I had to check the snow conditions above our high point for a summit attempt another year."

Reid returned to his wife and busy heart surgery practice in Diablo, California, and did not climb for two years. His next outing was a return to the East Face of Everest. This time he came fully prepared. He wore a formal kilt for the approach trek and had the "Little Engine that Could" embroidered on all of his climbing clothes. Reid, team doctor, was supposed to stay at base camp. However, no one on our team was surprised when Dan Reid reached the summit of Mount Everest on October 9, 1983, completing the first ascent of the Kangshung Face.

Everest was the culmination of thirty years of fanatical climbing that also included first ascents in Patagonia with Don Whillans, a solo ascent of the University Wall on Squamish Chief in 1969, the sixth ascent of the North American Wall on El Capitan in 1971, and the first ascent of the South Taku Tower in Alaska's Coast Range in 1973. But he was always fanatical about life.

Reid challenged the medical establishment with his frequent absences into the mountains. Yet he was such a good physician and surgeon, that he ascended the medical hierarchy to become a highly respected cardiothoracic surgeon. Intelligence and skill aside, it was his honesty, caring, and ability to give of himself that made Dan beloved by his patients, climbing partners, and friends from all walks of life. He was always upbeat. Even after forty-eight sleepless hours in the operating room he always had his silly grin and sense of humor. His laughter was infectious. He was genuinely excited about what his friends were doing. Then again, by most of our society's standards, Dan Reid was crazy.

He decided to run the Western States 100. No matter that he had never run more than ten miles at a single stretch and that to qualify one must have completed both a twenty-six-mile marathon and a fifty-mile race in good times within the previous year. Dan flew to New Orleans and ran his marathon. The next week he jetted to Baffin Island for a fifty-mile run that he finished just under the twelve-hour limit. Two weeks later Dan completed the Western States 100. He missed winning a silver beltbuckle for a time under twenty-four hours by only eighteen minutes. With a grin he related, "If I hadn't doubled up vomiting for an hour at mile seventy-six I could have made it."

Reid decided to learn how to play the bagpipes. He spent two months in Scotland practicing twelve hours a day under the tutelage of a master. He soon called me to play his bagpipe rendition of "Hava Nigila" over the phone, offering to entertain if I had a traditional Jewish wedding. He dove into flyfishing. On the river he became the embodiment of a Green Drake, or whatever the fish were feeding on that day. He tried polo. Soon Dan had a practice cage built onto his house, owned eleven ponies, and was housing a top player he brought up from Argentina.

At home he supported his wife, Barbara, a remarkable person in her own right, helping her realize her goals. Barb was a registered nurse who specialized in cardiac rehabilitation. With Dan's help she started her own fitness consulting business and became a leader in preventive medicine and sports medicine in her community. She was also an accomplished marathoner, running much faster than her husband, and a skilled horsewoman.

Dan was loyal to his friends. He was generous with his time, his skills, and his assets. He was also fiercely patriotic. Reid put his climbing career on hold in the early 1970's when America became involved in Vietnam. Dan did not simply sign up to be a military surgeon. He became a full-combat Green Beret. At age forty-nine, Reid left his lucrative cardiac surgery practice to join Operation Desert Storm. Despite the intensity of his actions, Reid was one of the most easy going, humorous, and fun people with whom I have shared a climbing rope. Don Whillans, who called Dan the "Mad American," loved to tell of the time Dan was leading a horrendous pitch of loose overhanging verglas in a raging storm in Patagonia. Whillans and the other British wanted to retreat. Dan smiled and said, "Come on! This isn't as bad as Vietnam!"

Dan Reid lived by the doctrine of "Cram as much into life as possible and maximize your fun doing it." He was chronically late from always trying to squeeze in one more thing. He had the courage to accept life's challenges and a zest for life itself. His real contribution, however, was his smile and the way he cared about people. His friends knew that he would be there if they needed him.

Seilschaft

DID DAN REID HAVE A DEATH-WISH? Do I have a death-wish? The answer to both questions is emphatically, no! It is a joy of life that we shared. Dan Reid exuded and savored life. An old Hindu expression states, "It is not how many Dawalis you have seen, but how many firecrackers you have lit." I say that it is more important to have lived much, than to have lived long. Dan Reid maximized his life. He was always willing to turn blind corners, face new challenges, and throw himself fully into every moment of his time on earth. I do feel sad about Dan's death and grieve that I will not be able to share more experiences with him. However, I would not want to change the way he lived his life, even if it would prolong his existence. Living life with passion is worth the risk. I do not believe in an after-life or reincarnation. But, I know that some of Dan Reid lives on in those of us who knew him. His spirit will be passed on to my children. This does not mean that I do not value life. On the contrary, facing death and having friends perish heightens my appreciation for life, makes me more cognizant of the small joys and pleasures of everyday living, and increases my desire to experience, feel, and savor every moment of my life. It also leaves me with a healthy level of fear when it is appropriate.

Taking risks, whether in the mountains, a career, or a relationship can be scary. I have had plenty of moments when I was afraid. However, I never became paralyzed by the terror. A knowledge of the possible consequences helps me to focus my concentration and increases my performance. There have been, however, times when I wished I were someplace else. One of my favorite old cartoon shows had a little turtle who was given the opportunity to experience various adventures. Invariably, he got into trouble. Each episode ended with him screaming, "Mr. Wizard! Mr. Wizard! I don't want to be a Knight of the Round Table any more!" Mr. Wizard would then say, "Dreezel, drizzle, drazzle, drome, time for this one to come home," and Tudor Turtle would be transported safely away just before the Black Knight's lance skewered him. Alas, no wizard exists for me. My cries of "Mr. Wizard, I don't want to be a mountaineer anymore!" have been in vain. I have had to rely on my own skills, a bit of luck, and my partners for survival.

I agree with Teddy Roosevelt when he said, "The credit belongs to the man who is in the arena; who strives valiantly; who errs and comes up short again; who knows the great enthusiasms; the great devotions; who, at the best, knows in the end the triumph of high achievement and who, at the worst, if he fails, at least fails while daring greatly, so that his place will never be with those timid souls who know neither victory nor defeat." I am grateful for the opportunity to share time with all of my partners, whether novices or experts, and whether we succeeded or failed. The most important thing is that we tried, and we shared the experience.

Sharing an adventure, and working together to survive, builds very tight bonds. All pretense is stripped away. There can be no facade or games. This allows great insights into both yourself and your partner. The intensity of these interpersonal experiences has led to many of my closest friendships. I had the privilege of spending an evening with Heinrich Harrer, the great adventurer whose writings changed my outlook on life. The spry octogenarian—who skied in the 1936 Olympics, made the first ascent of the Eiger Nordwand, spent "Seven Years in Tibet" and became a tutor and friend of the Dalai Lama, made important explorations and first ascents in Alaska and the Andes, was the first outsider to encounter the highland Dani, the first to penetrate to the Carstensz Range and the first to climb its major peaks—was warmly animated as he recounted anecdotes from his amazing life. I asked Heinrich what he felt were his most significant accomplishments. He instantly replied, "seilschaft," referring to the life-long bonds he formed with his partners who shared the experiences.

My feelings of "seilschaft" are also strong. The bond of the rope, where you mutually trust your life to your partner's skill and judgment, has created enduring friendships for me. The mountain relationship is totally honest. You know exactly what both you and your partner are capable of, and you must accept each other's limitations, and work together to succeed. This leads to a relationship based on acceptance and trust and produces long-term, caring, loyal friendships. I like my fellow adventurers and climbers. People who are willing to put themselves on the line and accept new risks are people whom I enjoy spending time with. Being with someone who is curious and expanding as a person pushes me to explore and learn more about the world and myself.

This self-expansion is where turning blind corners has led me. It has helped me to remain curious and realize that, as I learn more, there are no definite answers, only more questions. It is difficult to express the joy I get from climbing and adventures. People can point to the hardships and risks and question my use of the word "joy," but it is truly joy; joy in the discoveries, in the movement, in the situations, in the travel, in the views, in the successes on the summits, in the focussing of energy in failure, and in the seilschaft. I climb more than simply, "because it is there." I climb because I am here.

I am often asked, "What do you do after you have conquered the seven summits?" My first answer is that I never conquer a mountain. I have been lucky enough climb on some wonderful peaks and feel like a part of them for awhile. Second, there are enough new climbs and adventures for me to explore in this world for many more lifetimes. Finally, I try not to dwell on what I have accomplished, but concentrate on what I am doing now.

I remember Carlos Buhler saying, "The people who succeed and do not push on to a greater failure are the spiritual middle classes. Their stopping at success is proof of their compromising insignificance. How petty their dreams must have been." As for me, I still have plenty of dreams left to fail on.